# CULTURE CLASH

## H. NED SEELYE ■ ALAN SEELYE-JAMES

NTC Business Books

*NTC/Contemporary Publishing Group*

W9-DDY-999

**Library of Congress Cataloging-in-Publication Data**

Seelye, H. Ned.
    Culture clash : managing in a multicultural world / H. Ned Seelye.
Alan Seelye-James.
      p.   cm.
    Includes bibliographical references.
    ISBN 0-8442-3304-8 (hbk.)
    ISBN 0-8442-3306-4 (pbk.)
    1. Corporate culture.    2. Intercultural communication.
3. Multiculturism.    I. Seelye-James, Alan.    II. Title.
HD58.7.S43    1995
3023.3′5—dc20                           94-16177
                                       CIP

Published by NTC Business Books
A division of NTC/Contemporary Publishing Group, Inc.
4255 West Touhy Avenue, Lincolnwood (Chicago), Illinois 60646-1975 U.S.A.
Copyright © 1995 by H. Ned Seelye and Alan Seelye-James.
All rights reserved. No part of this book may be reproduced, stored in a retrieval
system, or transmitted in any form or by any means, electronic, mechanical,
photocopying, recording, or otherwise, without the prior permission of
NTC/Contemporary Publishing Group, Inc.
Printed in the United States of America
International Standard Book Number: 0-8442-3304-8 (cloth)
                                       0-8442-3306-4 (paper)

18    17    16    15    14    13    12    11    10    9    8    7    6    5    4    3

## Dedication
To Alfred E. Neuman, without whom Murphy would have become a crazed 600-pound gorilla.

# Acknowledgments

First and foremost, we acknowledge our debt to our clients, companions through thick and thin, in scores of countries.

Michael Seelye, whose opinion we value, read the first draft of this book and said he liked it. Several stalwart professionals read later versions of the manuscript: Anne Knudsen, executive editor of NTC Business Books, provided encouragement and insightful suggestions; Richard Hagle and Marcia Seidletz, able NTC editors, made salutary observations; Randy Nord, vice president of Kurt Salmon Associates, shared helpful comments; Clara James Seelye offered pertinent suggestions.

Friends and colleagues shared their experiences: Butch González; Catherine Bissel, who related the story of Juan Gutiérrez over lunch at the Saigonnais in Washington, D.C.; and others as well, some of whom are mentioned in the text.

Individuals who provided encouragement and support in various stages of the book include Colleen Bruner, Joy Montgomery, Virginia Armstrong, J. Laurence Day, Walter Galindo, María Cristina Gosserez Torres, Libby Morgan, David Seelye, Liz Wilson, and Jeff and Jenny Glenn, who throughout the process kept the engine stoked with coal. Many KSA colleagues offered encouragement.

Joe Durica of Durica Design (LaGrange Park, Illinois) prepared the book's internal graphics. The cover was designed by Scott Rattray.

# Contents

# Case Study Titles

# Case Study Titles

# Introduction

As we charge into the twenty-first century, the concept of a global economy rings sharper than ever, in alphabet code—EEC, NAFTA, GATT. The letters keep spilling out of our newspapers. Technological advances in travel and telecommunications have provided the means for accelerated integration of the world market.

Competition comes from every corner of the globe in today's marketplace and is forcing many businesses to look at new ways of cutting costs while maintaining market share and high quality levels. Businesses that had remained largely provincial have had local options narrowed and global options expanded. The low cost of labor and overhead available in foreign markets is encouraging many manufacturers to study the option of sourcing product offshore. In the past ten years there has been an increasing number of manufacturers doing just that, taking advantage of labor costs (several countries have hourly wages starting as low as 50 cents per hour) and other incentives (such as subsidized labor costs, or tax shelters) provided by their governments. It is not surprising that the study of foreign languages is on the rise.

Managers and consultants schooled in the ways of multinational businesses and multicultural service organizations are critical to the expansion of international opportunities. Glance at the job ads in big city newspapers. Opportunities are everywhere if you have the international skills. Saudi Arabia needs English-language teachers and rocket specialists. Chad seeks agricultural experts. A Washington, D.C., periodical advertised recently for an Albanian-speaking cosmetologist to bring the latest hairstyling techniques to Tiranë! Check out those hairstyles in a year or two.

A global economy is not a new thing. There has always been considerable trade across vast areas of the globe. In Neolithic times, business secrets, such as how to make cutting tools and ceramic or iron or bronze, spread across tribal boundaries at an average rate of slightly over one mile per year, according to one eminent anthropologist. In more recent—but still ancient—history, the pace of diffusion quickened. The hordes of Phoenicians, Babylonians, Mongols, Romans, Germanic tribes, Moors, Aztecs, Incas, et al. running about in pre-automobile days trying to improve their material wealth have ensured that trade with the "outside" world remains a driving force in the acquisition of goods and in the transfer of technology.

An example of this is the trade in curare, a poison put on darts and arrows that numbs the respiratory system just when the hunted animal needs increased oxygen to escape and causes suffocation. Amazon Indians trade curare across a jungle network of trading associates from many different tribes and product is finally consumed in an operating room in a hospital in Baltimore where it is used as a relaxant during chest operations.

Those boundaries of nation-states that snuggle up to neighbor states inspire lively commerce—in both smuggled and legally imported products. The Texas-Mexico border, to take one example, has been for many years one symbiotic economic zone extending for about fifty miles on either side of the border. Record levels of Christmas sales in McAllen, Texas, according to the local merchants, are due to the extended holiday season in Mexico, where people typically have two or three weeks of vacation. At any time of the year, the mall parking lots sport pickups and cars with Mexican license plates. To see U.S. plates, cross the river over to Reynosa, Mexico.

Business people have always been on the cutting edge of marketing the latest technological wonders—and not just technological wonders. Admiral Columbus was bankrolled by monied sponsors to open cheaper trade routes to satisfy the bored palates of European eaters.

This trend of internationalizing business and services has led to increasing numbers of people working in multicultural settings. Business relationships are being forced to overcome cultural differences as firms strive to maintain a competitive edge in the marketplace. This is not as easy as it sounds. Working in foreign countries is, as the name implies, an alien experience. This means language and, importantly, understanding diverse values in the workplace. Methods successful in one country's operations can and often do meet with failure when transplanted in another cultural setting. This book is replete with examples. Folks who are able to work effectively with international counterparts will be successful; those who do not deal with relevant cross-cultural issues will increase their vulnerability to economic "natural selection."

What is new about the global economy is its scale. Virtually everyone everywhere is affected by it, and about a quarter of the planet's people are directly affected. Many countries in the Middle East, Europe, and Asia import "guest workers" from other countries to satisfy industrial demands. Canada and the United States have experienced unprecedented immigration. Japanese immigrant farmers till rich soil in Brazil. These movements of people create multicultural residential neighborhoods and work settings. The children of these workers, professional and blue collar alike, turn our schools into international microcosms. More than 100 languages are spoken in schools in New York City, Chicago, Los Angeles, and Fairfax County, Virginia. According to April 1994 projections by the U.S. Census Bureau, by the year 2000, "minorities" will constitute the majority of the population in California, and by 2015, in Texas as well. "Minorities" are already the majority in Hawaii, New Mexico, and the District of Columbia. By the year 2020, the populations of Maryland, Arizona, New York, Nevada, and New Jersey will contain between 42 percent and 45 percent "minority" peoples. The majority of many cities in other states (Chicago is an example) is now "minority." The Hispanic and Asian populations are projected to encompass one-third of the U.S. population by the year 2050. Dealing across cultures has gone from being a take-it-or-leave-it proposition to being a prerequisite for survival—*your* survival.

In fact, you are going to be left behind if you do not acquire multicultural skills. In bygone days, assignments abroad often consigned the hapless but happy executive to oblivion. Today, you have a better shot at corporate advancement if you have extensive international experience.

It's a global economy and you'd better get with it—fast—if you want a piece of the action. The global market is like a breeder reactor, feeding on itself for energy. And it has reached critical mass. Partly in response to the enormous economic potential of the EEC (European Economic Community), the Western Hemisphere has negotiated NAFTA (North American Free Trade Agreement), eliminating trade barriers between Canada, the United States, and Mexico. Largely through Mexico's participation, other Central and South American countries will become beneficiaries, too. NAFTA is increasing business opportunities for its constituent nations. Capitalizing on these opportunities will require persons skilled in crossing cultural boundaries. Those who do not have these skills risk losing multimillion-dollar opportunities. Needless to say, international companies are anxious to find people with these skills. This book will help prepare you to become one of those people.

For an organization to incur the considerable cost of sending someone to work overseas, the person's technical and professional competency must be highly regarded. This book, therefore, does not concern itself with whether you know what you're talking about—it assumes you do. But can you communicate what you know? Can you get the information you need from the workplace to make wise recommendations? Can you establish rapport with local people? Can you get them to accept innovations that will increase productivity?

For anyone assigned to work overseas or to work with multiethnic peoples at home who speak a different language—both literally and figuratively—the first order of business is communication. This means understanding what people are *really* saying and getting your own message across in a way that will not put your physical well-being in harm's way.

The authors have focused *Culture Clash: Managing in a Multicultural World* on the practical problems commonly encountered in international consulting and management, but virtually anyone in any role in multicultural space will profit from reading it. The book deals with ways to increase accuracy in communication, to establish rapport with your coworkers, and to train people so that project sustainability is ensured. The book's objective is to help you, the intercultural voyager, become more effective on overseas projects and in multicultural work settings at home. This book will prepare you for multicultural environments, make you a better communicator, increase your awareness of the way cultures influence your interactions with others, and help you be more successful in your multicultural career.

Real-life cases from multicultural work settings in the United States, Europe, the former Soviet Union, Latin America, Asia, and Africa are presented and analyzed. Theoretical underpinnings are brought into play as they help the boundary crosser resolve blood-and-gut issues. To this end, we have included the kinds of details in more than forty cross-cultural incidents that provide a feel for the context within which multicultural voyagers operate. These cross-cultural incidents (some as brief as a paragraph, others several pages in length) are intrinsically fascinating. In some cases, to protect client confidentiality or the reputation of a particular manager or consultant (especially our own!), the authors have made appropriate changes in the accounts.

Not all of these examples come from the world of business managers and consultants, jet-setting to and fro. Researchers, teachers, trainers, volunteer social workers, students—all contribute to understanding how to survive international experiences. *Anyone* working or living in mixed cultural space—no matter what your level of multicultural experience has been—will find in this book something amusing and something thought-provoking.

# 1

# Coping with Culture Clash

Culture clash happens when people from two different cultures come into contact. Sometimes the clash begins before anyone has a chance to properly introduce you, before you even open your mouth. Culture clash can lead to world-class fatigue or even clinical shock or depression. Many of the adjustments to life in the cultural fast lane must be made early on, or the sojourner may become engulfed in anxiety and stress, preventing a successful overseas experience. Who suffers from culture clash? Everyone who spends much time with people from another culture.

## The Plight of the Sojourner

As an international voyager, perhaps as a manager or a consultant, you find yourself transplanted in a strange land, overwhelmed by a culture and a country that are foreign to you. You may have expected some roadblocks and even prepared yourself to work in a new environment. However, your success depends not only on working but also on living harmoniously within the community. In addition to dealing with another culture at work, before and after work you have to function in another culture, too. You are faced with coping and communicating twenty-four hours a day, seven days a week. This is fatiguing, and it can be devastatingly fatiguing. "What's wrong with me? Am I going crazy?" you wonder.

No, you're simply experiencing culture clash. Like the common cold, there is no medicine to cure it, but there are ways to mitigate the effects of culture clash so that you can still function.

What are the dastardly symptoms of culture clash? Is it contagious? Is it terminal? The following account reveals one real-life example of a virulent case of culture clash.

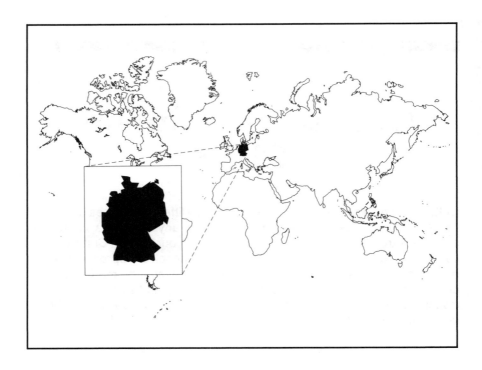

# THE PROFESSOR AND THE BABY CARRIAGE

A large-built Texan, a university professor of German, scheduled his sabbatical leave in Germany. He was enormously enthusiastic about the chance to do research in Germany, and the fact that he was going to be alone in a strange country hardly entered his mind. Upon arrival in Germany, the professor approached a number of people, mostly teachers and government officials, who he felt were in a position to help him survey the cultural beliefs of a sample of Germans. No one seemed very interested in his project. Each day he became more discouraged.

After several months of trying unsuccessfully to get his project off the ground, he began to blame others for their lack of interest and, worse, for their obstructionism; he felt the people he talked to were trying to undermine his efforts because he was an American. It was not long before he began to see Germans in general as the source of his frustration. Each day, his hostility increased. He would take his meals alone, then return to his room to brood about his failure. What was he going to tell his university colleagues back in Texas? How would he justify the paid sabbatical to his dean?

The breaking point came one afternoon several months later. He was walking down the street with his bulky briefcase in hand, when a German homemaker inadvertently blocked the sidewalk with her baby carriage. One more German obstructing his way! He became enraged and came within a fraction of striking the homemaker with his briefcase. His reaction so unnerved him that, out of fear of causing bodily injury, he kept himself locked up in his hotel room for the duration of the sabbatical, some six months.

## Analysis
### What happened?
Although the professor was fluent in German, he was not successful in launching his research, and he soon became hostile, then withdrawn.

### What really happened?
Differences in culture exacerbated the professor's routine frustrations. Conflict is present whenever two cultures come into contact. The conflict often results from a clash of values—a cultural difference in the perception of the appropriate way to get things done. Sometimes this conflict, played across the stage of daily interaction with people socialized in another culture, provokes strong physiological and psychological responses in the lonely, frustrated sojourner.

### What can the professor do now?
Unfortunately, he allowed his initial failure to find a mentor to overwhelm him. Had he been more persistent, he might have found someone who would have helped him develop a better approach to eliciting interest in his research topic or directed him to other, more interested, officials. Although embarrassed by these events, upon return to the United States he recovered his perspective of reality.

### How can this misunderstanding be avoided in the future?
One businessman, Igor Lelchitsky, discussing the dynamics of doing business in Russia, puts the initial phases of second-culture adjustment this way:

The first time you go to Russia you think you can do anything in the world. The second time, you start having your doubts. The third time, you think, "These Russians don't know what the hell they're doing." The fourth time, you think you don't know what the hell you're doing. (Reported by Don Steinberg in an article in *PC Computing*, Nov. 1990, p. 179.)

Most cases of culture clash are not as severe as the professor experienced. More generally, guests in another culture suffer from psychological weariness rather than from outright shock. Getting through the daily routine is so much more tiring in another culture!

---

# Defining Culture Clash

This phenomenon that results from a clash in cultures was called *culture shock* over thirty-five years ago by Kalervo Oberg, an anthropologist. V. Lynn Tyler, a specialist in intercultural communication, prefers the terms *self-discovery shock*, *role shock*, and *transition shock*. Whatever you call it, says Tyler, it all concerns dealing with diversity. *Culture fatigue* has been suggested by many as a more accurate description of what usually occurs. At the end of a day of dealing with myriad new cultural patterns, you are worn out. Jacqueline Howell Wasilewski, an intercultural communication specialist teaching at the International Christian University in Tokyo, approaches culture fatigue from a fresh perspective. "Too much is made of it," she says. "Of course you get tired. You are learning new things and all learning is fatiguing."

The symptoms of culture shock include a preoccupation with personal cleanliness and disease and dirt (and an inordinate fear of drinking the water and eating the food), a sense of being cheated, irritability with little provocation, hypersensitivity to perceived criticisms, and depression. Many suggest that there is an ebb and flow to these symptoms; culture clash is greater at some junctures than at others. Curves of various forms that represent rising and falling emotional intensity across time have been hypothesized. Some see a "U-curve," with a steady depression that plateaus after a year or two, then steadily gets better as one adjusts to life under different ground rules. Others see a "J-curve," with things turning sour soon after arrival in another culture, but improving steadily once you are over the hump. Some add a wrinkle by talking about a "W-curve," which is really two U-curves, with the second U referring to problems the sojourner often experiences when reentering his or her home culture.

There are five or six generally recognized stages of culture shock: the preliminary stage (events that occur before departure); the spectator phase (the initial weeks or months of living in another culture); the increasing participation phase; the shock phase; and the adaptation phase. Some add a sixth phase, the reentry into your home culture. Incidentally, an excellent literary source that helps these phases come alive was edited by Lewis and Jungman (see bibliography at the end of the book). These editors present four or five short pieces by major authors (for example, Camus, Conrad, Borges) organized under each of the six phases of culture shock.

Sojourners suffer from the inevitable malaise of cross-culturally induced fatigue for a number of reasons. The fatigue is occasioned by energies spent in an exaggerated concern for hygiene, by having to work harder to do simple things such as use the telephone or catch a bus, or by the constant irritation of dealing with people who "don't know how to get things done." All those who venture abroad for any lengthy stay contract it. Most recover within a few years, but recovery is gradual. It makes little difference whether the sojourner is an American terrified by the traffic patterns of Guatemala or a Guatemalan perspiring with claustrophobic anxiety in the subways of New York City. Culture fatigue is not a respecter of persons.

## Whose Reality Are We Talking About?

People of one culture experience difficulty observing the same "reality" as natives of another culture. Linguistically, for example, the inability of many Chinese to distinguish between the pronunciation of *reef* and *leaf* or the problems English-speakers have differentiating the Spanish *bata* from *pata* or *pero* from *perro*, or the difficulty of speakers of Spanish in distinguishing the two English words *frilly* and *freely*.

When dealing with a culture other than our own, we are not unlike John, who went blind shortly after birth but fortunately regained his sight at the age of 16. One of his major adjustments, he related, was to learn not to see the inconsequential objects that came into his line of vision. While looking at a person across the room, for instance, everything within eyesight would demand equal visual attention. Our culture teaches us what to see and what to ignore. A newly arrived foreigner does not know what to see, let alone what to say.

An overriding element that provokes much cross-cultural fatigue, according to Harry Triandis, a social psychologist specializing in intercultural communication, is the way different cultures organize experience into different categories. Triandis gives the example of how Greeks define in-groups and out-groups. In-groups are formed of family and close friends. Greeks often extend the possibility of in-group membership to foreigners by asking the sort of question that one only asks, in Greece, of in-group members: "How much did that cost?" "How much money do you make?" If the foreigner is reluctant to answer questions that are "too personal," he or she may be forgoing unwittingly the proffered acceptance as a friend.

## The Strains of Culture Clash

Each of us experiences difficulties as we attempt to function effectively in another culture. Juan Gutiérrez, introduced in the next chapter, is just one sobering case in point. Richard Brislin and his colleagues at the East-West Center at the University of Hawaii identify many areas that are associated with the strains of cross-cultural adjustment. These include the following difficulties:

- *Dealing with anxiety whose origins are typically vague.* Brooding about their feelings leads sojourners to incorrect conclusions concerning their bind. Often the anxiety is produced by a loss of control over goal attainment (that is, needs satisfaction). You can get what you want so much easier in your own hometown.

- *Learning new culturally appropriate behaviors when sojourners may feel free of the constraints and social sanctions of their native culture.* The difficulty lies in missing the behavior that is appropriate to goal attainment in the second culture and, instead, engaging in behaviors that are atypical to both cultures.

- *Putting memorable events into proper perspective.* Emotionally charged personal experiences, especially if they are negative, can take on a significance that misrepresents the host culture. This tendency is exacerbated when one has a strong expectation that the experience violates.

- *Exercising the level of social skills needed to belong to host networks at a time when the sojourner is cut off from his or her support networks back home.*

- *Having to make decisions based on less information than one is accustomed to.*

- *Adjusting to different beliefs about how the workplace should be organized.* How is authority exercised? How much planning should precede action? How are incentives, rewards, and control effected? How much conformity and initiative are expected? What constitutes an appropriate work setting? How does gender affect expectations?

- *Recognizing how time is broken down in the host culture.* Brislin states that "the working unit of time for the Euro-American is the five-minute block." Some cultures have other "units." In the Arab and Hispanic business worlds, for instance, a fifteen-minute (or longer) block may reign.

- *Understanding the meaning of an ambiguous statement, such as "Let's have lunch together sometime."* Is the speaker just being polite or should a date be set?

- *Learning to feel comfortable with the greater or lesser physical distance that is observed between people in the host culture.* In Latin America this distance is typically six to twelve inches closer than is customary in the United States.

- *Recognizing new cues to role and how one is expected to interface with that role.* Some of the roles are novel (Guardian of the Beauty Path, an honored responsibility among some Native American tribes); others appear to be familiar but are defined differently (*executive* in Japan and the United States, for instance). A related area is how the pecking order is established and how status is apportioned.

- *Adjusting to sex roles that go against one's principles.* American females frequently have particular difficulty with behavior they classify as "sexist," aspects of Islamic or Hispanic cultures, for example.

These are some of the stresses and strains that feckless voyagers of multicultural space are personally subject to as they go about their business.

# Patience, patience . . .

All this learning of new ways to act takes a while to acquire. Whether we were raised to be multicultural and have had the task of mastering behaviors from multicultural roots since the beginning or whether we become multicultural later in our lives, it takes years to develop this adeptness. The learning curve has some dicey moments inherent in the process—imitation, fierce conservation of earlier behavior, denial of new and old behavior, sometimes in a totally mixed-up struggle for "supremacy," and rather exciting periods of serendipity and innovation.

One of the book's authors, Ned, spent several years researching the extent to which U.S. citizens living in Guatemala had acquired knowledge of Guatemalan culture patterns and the extent to which they had integrated themselves into Guatemalan social life. The bottom line is that it takes about five years, depending on the nature and extent of your contact with local people. It was not until after fifteen years of residence in Guatemala that the Americans were indistinguishable from the Guatemalans in terms of their knowledge and social interactions. If the contrast between the two cultures is even greater than that between the United States and Guatemala, it may take even longer. One American, presently residing in Japan, believes she will be 90 before she can read a newspaper like a normal Japanese 15-year-old.

This does not mean you have to wait five years to enjoy life in a culturally strange setting. You can have fun and be effective right from the start. But just as you check out what inoculations you may need to ward off the local microbes, you will do yourself a favor by checking out the perils of culture clash before you enter the murky waters without a paddle.

The rewards of multicultural space are beguiling. They enrich our lives with drama, stimulating memories, wonderful friends, deepened perspectives. The rewards invite all of us to pack our bags and hit the road to high adventure, *now.*

# 2

# Leaping the
# Language Barrier

The most foreign thing about a foreign place is the foreign language. Since communication is not an expendable skill for international managers and consultants, unless you are willing to limit your professional life to places that speak your language, you have four choices: throw silver dollars into a really good wishing well, play charades, use interpreters, or learn the language.

## The Saga of Juan Gutiérrez

One story, perhaps not completely true, will set the stage for a discussion of the travails of communication through interpreters.

A Mexican bandit rides across the Rio Grande and robs a bank in a sleepy Texas border town, then heads back to Mexico. Bank officials rush to find the marshal, but he is out of town. The deputy marshal is located, told of the crime, and given a description of the bandit: brown eyes, medium height, wearing a black poncho and, incongruously, a white ten-gallon hat. He was riding a dapple-gray horse. "Look!" the bank clerk shouted. "There he goes now. You can still see him in the distance!"

The deputy rides out of town in pursuit. He crosses the Rio Grande, rides over hill and dale, but can't seem to close the gap separating him from the bandit. He loses sight of the bandit when the culprit enters a small Mexican town. Twenty minutes later the deputy reaches the town. There, in front of the *cantina*, a lone horse is tethered. A dapple-gray. From the sweat, he could tell that the horse was recently "rode hard." The deputy pushes the swinging doors aside and enters. Leaning against the bar is a brown-eyed Mexican cowboy of medium height, dressed in a black poncho. His head is capped by a white ten-gallon *sombrero*.

The deputy strides up to the lone patron and asks him whether he speaks English.

"No, señor," responds the perspiring patron.

"Bartender," asks the deputy, "do you speak English?"

"Sí, señor," responds the bartender.

"Ask this man whether he has just returned from Los Mudos, Texas."

The bartender translates.

"No," replies the perspiring patron.

"He say, 'No,' " translates the bartender.

The deputy unholsters his Colt, presses the barrel against the profusely perspiring patron's temple, and addresses the bartender.

"You tell him that if he doesn't tell me right now where the money is hidden, he will never live to enjoy another tequila sunset."

The bartender translates.

The bandit, shaken, tells the bartender that he hid it behind doña Rosa's house, in the woodpile.

The bartender turns to the deputy and translates. "He say, 'Juan Gutiérrez is prepared to die.' "

It's an old army cliché to say (with some irony) that "What we have here is a failure to communicate." Communication problems are at the heart of many—maybe most—human dramas.

When working through interpreters, conflicting vested interests are not the only problem. A survey conducted by David Ricks and Michael Czinkota revealed that U.S. firms ranked communication as number 1 out of 33 major international problem areas.

When working internationally you will be in a situation in which

- you are talking to someone who does not speak any language you speak, but you have an interpreter.

- you are talking to someone with whom you do not share a common language, but you do not have an interpreter.

- the person speaks a shared language, but as a second language with only a marginal level of fluency.

And sometimes you will interact with a person who speaks a shared language fluently.

Interpreters can alter substantially the tone of the message. It can come out overly harsh or too diplomatic. Four real-life incidents illustrate this.

A Japanese consultant delicately explained, in English, the costs and repercussions of their current system of inadequate quality controls to upper management (including the person responsible for quality control) in a German-speaking group working in southern Brazil. The CEO translated the lengthy discourse in one sentence: "The man says our quality is shit!"

In another setting, Paul, a U.K. manager working in Russia, was furious. He stormed into the Russian plant director's office to ask why he had changed the incentive scheme they had agreed upon. Paul did this using sharp words. The interpreter translated the "sense" of this message while hiding the fervent displeasure it contained. Jeff was present during this exchange and later asked the interpreter about her translation. She explained that she usually softened biting comments, because she was embarrassed to be speaking to a plant director in such a way.

If time and resources allow, learning the language is preferable and can reap both personal and professional benefits, as Jeff discovered during an assignment in Siberia. He had been in the factory less than a month when his birthday made its annual appearance. To Jeff's surprise, the people he worked with chartered a boat and took him out on the river that flowed by the city. That evening on the boat he was treated to homemade Russian cuisine and heartfelt Russian songs. At one point, Jeff asked the head trainer whether it was the custom to entertain all of the foreign specialists so lavishly.

The trainer leaned toward the specialist's ear and replied, "We've never done this for someone we had to work with through interpreters" (although non-Russian-speaking people of high status occasionally are accorded this honor by plant directors).

If achieving language proficiency is not possible, then you must rely on interpreters. And you can do so successfully, as in the case of Jo Taylor, a U.K. consultant working in Kenya. Although she did not speak Swahili, the lingua franca of most of the workforce, she was able to communicate well through an interpreter. Jo had made a special effort to develop an especially good relationship with her interpreter. She briefed her in advance of sessions and debriefed her after sessions to get a better sense of the nuances of communication. Jo also extended social courtesies by giving little presents for the birthdays of the interpreter's children.

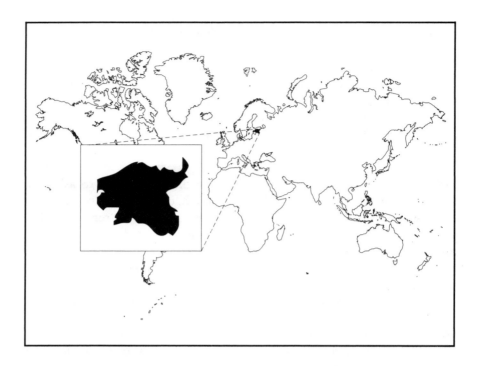

## TRANSLATING THE INSCRUTABLE

One English engineer, Diana Jones, was working on an engineering project in Estonia shortly before its separation from the former Soviet Union.
The Soviet government was in the midst of implementing its plan for
restructuring the economy (*perestroika*) and, consequently, was investing
in revamping numerous industries with Western technology. The objective of the project was to modernize this electronic facility to be competitive with Western equivalents.

The Estonian management, sensitive to ''political correctness'' in
an increasingly nationalistic state, preferred to converse in Estonian, although Russian was the official language. Most communication that occurred between the consulting group and the Estonians was done through
interpreters.

At one point, Diana described a plan for increasing production and
improving quality with state-of-the-art equipment and by working in

modules (teams in which a worker does more than one operation and checks the work of the previous operation). Diana presented the plan to management, estimating the gains in production and quality that would be reaped by using the new equipment and from cross-training the modular teams. Diana's presentation went something like this:

"Now that we have the new soldering equipment we should be able to attach the transistors in one-third the time. This alone should give us an increase in the production of this model of eight percent. By setting up modules of 13 people apiece and cross-training them, we can reduce waiting time from five percent to below one percent. The cross-training will take somewhere between eight and twelve weeks. More important, we can reduce DHUs (defects per hundred units) from 7 percent to 0.5 percent with each worker checking the others' quality. The combined result should be an increase of 15 percent in overall production levels."

Diana, excited by the potential gains, observed an unimpressed Estonian management.

## Analysis
### *What happened?*
The interpreter did not translate accurately. She had mistakenly translated *transistor* as *resistor*. Understanding the intended meaning of this was fundamental to accepting the plan. The interpreter also botched the translation of *module* and *cross-training*. The result was a confused and skeptical Estonian management.

### *What really happened?*
The interpreters who were used had an in-depth background in colloquial English and in the English of classic literature, but they were not familiar with much of the technical terminology peculiar to the electronics industry. This gap in their knowledge led to many communication problems. Because the interpreter was not familiar with industrial issues and engineering terms, she sought rough equivalents and circumlocutions to explain what she herself did not understand. The results were jagged, as this example illustrates.

### *What can Diana do now?*
First, find out what the management does and does not understand. Then clarify the understanding of the interpreter by explaining terms

such as *modules*, *cross-training*, and *DHUs*. In the follow-up presentation to management, use simple language while pointing to graphics depicting the key concepts.

### How can this misunderstanding be avoided in the future?

Trying to obtain the services of interpreters/translators who understand the technical field is the best hedge. Even then, however, the following tips will help you to achieve an accurate understanding.

---

| TOOLBOX |

## How to Use Interpreters Effectively

- Use simple words. Avoid slang and idiomatic expressions. Keep each point brief and straightforward.

- When the message you are communicating is complex, go over it with the interpreter beforehand to ensure the interpreter has a clear understanding of what you want to communicate.

- Encourage the interpreter to keep you informed of any discussion that takes place within the group. This will help you keep the discussion on track.

- Use graphics to help you convey key concepts.

- Watch the group and listen to the group's replies. Even though you may not understand what they are saying, there will be plenty of nonverbal communication that can reinforce the translation when you receive it.

- Find out something about the culture in which you will find yourself. Reading books about the host country's culture and talking to someone who has worked in the country can be quite helpful.

- Have a short debriefing session with the interpreter because he or she may have picked up some messages that were not translated. Problems can arise if the manager or consultant is unaware of conversations that took place in the meeting which were not translated. The translator is in a good position to interpret the host people's attitudes and the intrusion of hidden agendas.

- Before the meeting, give your interpreter a brief written overview of what you are going to say during the meeting.

- Briefly summarize, orally and in writing, after each meeting and have it translated by the interpreter who was present. This summary can then be circulated to those who were at the meeting to reinforce their understanding.

# Using Translators and Interpreters

The consequences of miscommunicated business concepts are often hilarious—and costly. An infamous example of forgetting to review your product's name prior to launching an ad campaign in another country is that of General Motors when it was promoting the automobile Nova in Latin America. In Spanish, Nova means "doesn't go" (*no va*), and it did not take long for Latin American consumers to smile, shake their heads, and say, *no va*. Examples of similar foul-ups include Ford's Pinto (Portuguese for "small male appendage"), and Colgate's Cue (an obscenity in French). They all faced the difficulty of having a name with an undesirable connotation, as did the Finnish beer "Koff" and the French manufacturer Bich (now Bic) in English-speaking countries.

Sometimes advertising is translated in corporate headquarters by someone who has an overly literal mind, or who is not familiar with the target culture. These are a few examples of what happens when you ask for verbatim translations. Roger E. Axtell in *Do's and Taboos of Hosting International Visitors* recounts many of these bloopers. Pepsi-Cola's "Come Alive with Pepsi" ad campaign was translated for Taiwan as "Pepsi brings your ancestors back from the grave." A neat trick. And a Swedish manufacturer used the slogan "Nothing sucks like an Electrolux" to promote its vacuum cleaners in the English-speaking world. This slogan proved unusable in the United States, where it means, in slang, that the vacuum cleaners were of terrible quality. The slogan also carried obscene overtones in the U.S. market. When General Motors entered the Belgian market, it mistranslated its slogan "Body by Fisher" into Flemish as "Corpse by Fisher."

Axtell advises business people to seek out professional translators when a professional job is needed. Two national professional translation associations in the United States include the American Association of Language Specialists in Washington, D.C., and The American Translators Association in Ossining, New York. Other sources can be found in the local telephone directory of major cities.

There are alternatives to using interpreters, however. There are charades.

One manager, with a limited knowledge of Russian, regularly spent weekends with the family of the production manager. Neither spoke more than a handful of words in the other's language. They often would have barbecues on the river bank. Through sign language they would agree on who would get the wood, cut the cucumbers, cut the tomatoes, and do the other required chores. This relationship helped them talk to each other back at the plant through an interpreter.

# Learning the Language

Since many of the communication problems described in this chapter could have been avoided if the hero or heroine had had a better understanding of the local language, let us look at this option a little closer.

There is no question that in the best of all possible worlds, it is far better if you speak the language. This will demonstrate to others your commitment to communicate, and this in turn will put you in a better position to do so effectively. Over the years, international managers and consultants often work in dozens of language areas, but becoming really fluent in the local language is not always possible or practical. There are just too many languages.

Should you or shouldn't you expend the time and effort to learn the host language? Should you spend time training the workforce in your language, or should you rely on interpreters and hope to fare better than Juan Gutiérrez? Sometimes you may run into a language that relatively few people speak. Ned worked on a training project in a tiny Amazon Indian village of twenty seminomadic families who spoke a distinct language—a language that was shared by only 500 people in the world. What do you do in that situation? (He worked through one of the few villagers who spoke a shared language, Spanish.)

Even if you choose to train the workforce in your language and use an interpreter, it is always helpful to learn some of the language. Boye Lafayette De Mente, a specialist in Asian customs, notes that even a small amount of ability in the language will go a long way in helping to make and sustain the kind of personal relations needed to function effectively. And this ability is not limited just to conducting business itself, but in greetings, casual comments, at eating and drinking parties, and so on. Time constraints will determine the language training you receive, but it is always best to learn as much as you can—even if you will be in the host country for only a short visit. Social courtesies are appreciated, and learning a few phrases counts as one of them. Companies would do well to budget time and funds for language training for their managers who will be working in a country for six months or more when they do not speak the language. The time and money invested in language training quickly pays for itself.

How do you determine how to deal with the language barrier? You must first determine in what capacity you will use the language and what may be the cost of a communication breakdown. Are you planning to develop a long-term relationship with a client? Or will you only be on-site for one week or two months? If you are ill equipped linguistically for the assignment, is there someone with the required technical skills who is better equipped linguistically? Or is it you or nobody? The answers to these questions will help you determine what direction you should take.

Developing competency in any foreign language is, for most of us, a demanding task. There are, however, some shortcuts. In languages within the same language family (for example, Spanish, French, Portuguese, and Italian), many words originate from the same source in the older shared language (Latin). (Linguists call words that share a common root *cognates*.) This is a big aid in learning the language. Some years ago in the interior of Brazil, the head of a school listened in awe at the more or less intelligible Portuguese-sounding speech emanating from the mouth of a visitor from the U.S. Then the director's face lit up, and with an admiring smile he told Ned that his skill in "Portuguizing" Spanish produced a *mata galihna* (chicken-killing) lingo. "What do you mean, chicken killing?" "Well," the director replied, "you'll never die of hunger in Brazil."

Even languages that are not related—for example, English and Japanese—borrow words from other languages. The Japanese word *besuboru* for the popular American sport of baseball is an example. Other shortcuts are listed by Douglas Brown in his excellent book, *Breaking the Language Barrier*.

---

## ┃TOOLBOX┃

# Assessing the Cost of Not Speaking the Language

What is the risk of . . .

| | Low | | | | High |
|---|---|---|---|---|---|
| Losing the contract? | 1 | 2 | 3 | 4 | 5 |
| Losing key employees? | 1 | 2 | 3 | 4 | 5 |
| Losing considerable production? | 1 | 2 | 3 | 4 | 5 |
| Losing quality? | 1 | 2 | 3 | 4 | 5 |
| You being replaced? | 1 | 2 | 3 | 4 | 5 |
| Losing critical baseline data? | 1 | 2 | 3 | 4 | 5 |
| Losing support of locals? | 1 | 2 | 3 | 4 | 5 |
| Other cost of misunderstanding: | | | | _____?: | |
| | 1 | 2 | 3 | 4 | 5 |

If you score in the 4 or 5 range on any dimension, your risk is high enough to consider taking special steps to avoid miscommunication. There are three things to consider: the level of professionalism of your interpreter (including the extent to which he or she commands the technical understanding that the project requires); the number of interpreters you will use; and the manner in which you will deploy the interpreters (in relief shifts, simultaneously—one to check the other; for both written and oral language use).

For oral communications, you may want to use a professional interpreter instead of a local person who happens to speak your language. (And here, Juan Gutiérrez would wholeheartedly agree.) There is a big difference between speaking two languages fluently and being able to translate proficiently—quickly and accurately—between them. For highly critical written communications, you may consider using two translators, one to translate into the host language and the other to translate back into the original language. This enables you to verify the accuracy of the translation and to pinpoint any difficulties.

One startling discovery made by Raymond Gorden, a sociologist studying miscommunication between visitors from the United States and Colombians, was that misunderstandings between the U.S. visitors and their hosts were greater when the visitors were more fluent than average in Spanish. The U.S. visitors who spoke hesitantly with a heavy accent were misunderstood less. The reason? The Colombians assumed that the fluent visitors who sounded as though they knew what they were talking about *did* know what they were talking about. Unfortunately, they rarely did, for they had not been socialized into Hispanic life. They had acquired fluency in Spanish in a U.S. cultural setting. Their cultural referents were U.S., not Hispanic.

Why didn't the U.S. visitors who murdered the language get into more communication difficulties? Because when they spoke their halting Spanish, they didn't sound as if they knew much. Consequently, the Colombian hosts assumed ignorance of everything, including many basic Colombian cultural assumptions. The Colombians worked harder to understand these innocents abroad.

Even when you think you know the language (even when it's your native language!), you may still have language problems. A United Nations consultant from England still recalls his first visit to the United States. He arrived at a hotel in New York, checked in and asked the attractive clerk if he could get a wake-up call at six the next morning. He requested this by asking: "Would you knock me up at six?" The clerk was not amused. (In colloquial American English, *knock up* means to impregnate.)

As the earlier examples illustrate, understanding spoken words is only part of the communication process. Each person, inevitably, bases his or her interpretations of events on personal experiences which are filled with largely unconscious values, beliefs, and assumptions.

The guidelines suggested in this chapter will help to minimize miscommunication. This will take you a step closer to a successful overseas assignment. However, we must recognize that clear communication is a means to the end, but it is not the end. There are other factors that will influence the ultimate "success" of an undertaking and subsequent chapters deal with many of them.

When you do not have the time to learn the language, you can still learn a lot from nonverbal signs. Some communication specialists say that 70 percent or more of communication is nonverbal. Just like language, nonverbal communication is dependent on cultural contexts. Consequently, wait for the whole message (verbal + nonverbal + context) and if they conflict, check your understanding. More on this in the next chapter.

# 3

# Cracking the Silent Code

## *Communicating Across Different Values*

Anyone who has ventured into a developing nation discovers pretty quickly that time is conceptualized differently from what is the norm among industrialized people. Commonplace roles are defined differently from culture to culture. The amount of space people leave between themselves and others is culturally determined. The way people dress often conveys specific messages, and ignoring them, as a U.S. supervisor did on one painful occasion, can lead to severe foot-in-mouth maladies. This chapter examines these and other examples of The Silent Code—the cultural assumptions and values that underpin our behavior.

## Dealing with the Unspoken Aspects of Culture

Our grandfathers used to carry impressive gold watches in a special little pocket in their trousers. (Our grandmothers used nonindustrial systems to relate to time.) Nowadays, we get to the minute-hand quicker: it is on our wrist, either going round and round or blinking in a high-tech display.

## WHAT TIME DOES YOUR WATCH SAY?

It was a humid afternoon in Monterrey, an industrial city in northern Mexico where the inhabitants have earned the reputation for being slow

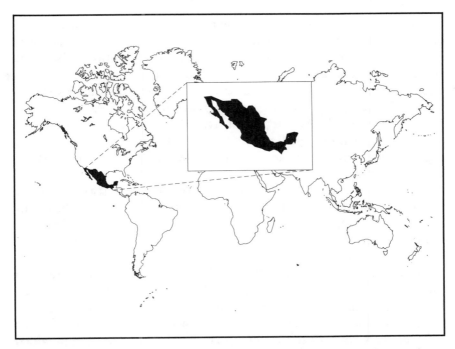

to part with their pesos. The air seemed to wear on the American trainer, David, like a layer of thermal clothing. The Human Resource Manager of the multimillion-dollar Mexican company, Licenciado (his academic title) Enrique Díaz, called the trainer into his office to tell him that the plant director wanted them to make a presentation.

"David, the Director wants us to make a presentation the day after tomorrow to the rest of management about how the training program will work."

"We have to get together beforehand to discuss what we need to include in the presentation. We need to review this today or tomorrow, then," responded David.

"I'm busy today. How about if I call you tomorrow morning to let you know when we can get together?" replied Enrique.

"That will be fine," agreed David. "I'll talk to you tomorrow."

The American trainer had been contracted to install an advanced analytical method of training (AAMT) program to train 120 operators to perform the operations that go into making television sets. These operations ranged from performing simple assembly line operations to working expensive electronically controlled injection molding machines.

It was late the following morning and Enrique had not called. Anxious to review the presentation material, David tried to call Enrique. Unfortunately, the luckless trainer could not locate Enrique. Since the two plants were in the process of being built (as a joint venture with a U.S. firm) the engineering and human resource departments were spread among five temporary locations throughout the area. Locating Enrique was not an easy task. At this point David was clearly frustrated. He was raised in an environment in which punctuality and promptness were highly valued. He had great difficulty understanding how any business could be run without these values.

David called Enrique's office again on the untrustworthy rotary phone and got a busy signal. He tried several more times before he finally got through— only to discover that Enrique was not there. David left a message with Enrique's secretary for him to return the call.

Finally, Enrique returned the call at four o'clock. He profusely apologized for his tardiness and unavailability. He asked the trainer to meet him at his office at six-thirty to review the presentation format. By then he would be finished with the meeting he was presently attending.

Six-thirty arrived and no Enrique. Seven-thirty came and David left. Irritated, he went back to the house that the conglomerate had provided for his stay. The only bright spot of the day for David was eating the delicious tacos that María del Carmen, the live-in housekeeper, made for dinner. Feeling refreshed, his outlook became more optimistic—at least the meeting didn't start until five o'clock the next afternoon. Surely, with the help of Enrique, he would have enough time to practice the Spanish he would need for the presentation.

The following morning David awoke to a dark and stormy day. The morning was spent trying to track down Enrique. No success here. Late in the afternoon David went to Enrique's office in the hope of running into his *compadre*. Four-thirty arrived like a French guillotine and Enrique, like a decapitated head, fell into his office. Enrique nervously chain-smoked as the two rushed to make overhead transparencies. At five o'clock they were informed through a third party that the meeting had been delayed until five-thirty. At that point, Enrique pulled out some overheads that David's firm had used to sell the training project to Enrique's boss, and he asked David to present them.

"But I've never seen them before," David said.

"That's all right. These went over big before. The Director was really impressed," said Enrique.

David looked over the overheads and noted there were several parameters he didn't understand very well.

David tried to talk him out of using the mysterious overheads, but Enrique insisted he use the overheads that had such stylish graphs.

Five-thirty came and there was another change in the schedule. The meeting had been shifted to another building. The meeting finally started at 7:00 P.M., but the Director never showed up. The plant managers and fifteen middle managers attended. Although David muffed a number of Spanish words, the presentation was well received.

Later in the project, David experienced similar irritation over punctuality while conducting training sessions with the plant engineers. During the first week of class, David noticed that several participants regularly arrived late at the sessions. This behavior clashed strongly with David's sense of the importance of punctuality. He made a point of lecturing them on the importance of punctuality and how it was important for them to exhibit the same qualities they would expect from their workers. This did not seem to help very much.

# Analysis
## *What happened?*
The problem David experienced involves the concept of time and its role in industry. David could not get his coworkers to respond to his respect for punctuality.

## *What really happened?*
David was beginning to learn that his Mexican colleagues did not feel the same sense of urgency regarding time commitments that is felt by the U.S. business community where "time is money." In the United States and other highly industrialized nations, verbal time commitments are binding, and it is a sign of irresponsibility or contempt to breach these commitments. This clashes with the Mexican view of time commitments. There, time commitments are viewed as desirable goals, but they are not binding. Besides, circumstances change and what today is considered a good idea for a future get-together may not seem as high a priority tomorrow. Whatever isn't done today can always wait until *mañana*, God willing (*si Dios quiere*).

Cultural factors affect how you interpret time. The closer a country is to its agrarian roots, the more it tends to measure time in terms of diurnal and seasonal changes. A clock doesn't tell you if it will soon be dark; you look at the position of the sun. This view of time doesn't work well in many if not most industrial settings where smaller units of time take on a new relevance. In many countries the transition to industrial time occurs gradually as greater productivity and on-time service become more of an issue in the workplace.

David learned that in the plant where he was consulting the typical working hours were from nine o'clock to six o'clock. It was not uncommon for the engineers to work late into the night. (David's first erroneous conclusion when he noticed this was that they were avoiding going home to their families.) Given this work pattern, it is understandable that they were frequently tardy for early morning sessions. Then too, the engineers were told to arrive at the training sessions at 8:30, but they were not compensated for this extra time.

### What could David do in that situation?

David did talk to the engineers about the situation, but that did not alter their behavior.

### How can this misunderstanding be avoided in the future?

First, *understand the dynamics*. Time anywhere in the world is generally viewed from some point on a continuum, with "monochronic" time at one end and "polychronic" time at the other. Monochronic time approaches time in a linear fashion. In this system things are dealt with one at a time in an orderly fashion. Industrial settings are usually organized in this fashion. Polychronic time involves doing a number of things at once, weaving them together in a dynamic process that considers changing circumstances. Traditional village life in much of the world operates this way.

When people from two different time systems interact, both parties typically experience frustration. And the frustration can be acute.

A sense of monochronic time pervades North American and northern European cultures. In these cultures time is treated as a precious commodity that can be saved, wasted, or lost. In the United States, grade school teachers tell children not to waste time. This parallels Benjamin Franklin's business refrain: Time is money. In monochronic time systems, schedules are strictly followed, and punctuality and promptness are highly valued. Adherence to schedules also makes a statement about the status and importance of the person.

In many countries, Mexico included, the general and the workplace culture often are based on polychronic time, rather than on Mickey Mouse time. For adherents of polychronic time, commitments are objectives, but not etched-in-stone commandments. They prefer meetings or conversations to end in a natural conclusion, rather than one that has a time limit as dictated by a schedule. (And, following this logic, it is considered bad form to state on a social invitation the anticipated ending time.)

Second, *understand yourself*. Although an awareness of cultural differences does not always eliminate frustration, it takes you a step closer to understanding what's happening. Edward and Mildred Hall, in *Understanding Cultural Differences*, list some characteristics common to monochronic people and polychronic people.

---

## TOOLBOX

## Assessing Your Orientation to Time

How **monochronic** are you? Check the statements that fit.

- ☐ Like to do one thing at a time.
- ☐ Concentrate on the job at hand.
- ☐ Take time commitments (deadlines, schedules) seriously.
- ☐ Am committed to the job.
- ☐ Adhere closely to plans.
- ☐ Am concerned about not disturbing others (follow rules of privacy).
- ☐ Show great respect for private property (seldom borrow or lend).
- ☐ Emphasize promptness in meetings.
- ☐ Am comfortable with short-term relationships.

Or perhaps you have **polychronic** traits. Check the statements that fit.

- ☐ Like to do many things at once.
- ☐ Am highly distractible and frequently interrupt what I am doing.

☐ Consider time commitments more of an objective to be achieved, if possible, than a quasi-legal contract.

☐ Am committed to people and human relationships.

☐ Change plans often and easily.

☐ Put obligations to family and friends before work concerns.

☐ Intimacy with family and friends is more important than respecting their privacy.

☐ Borrow and lend things often and easily.

☐ Base the level of promptness on the particular relationship.

☐ Have a strong tendency to build lifetime relationships.

Most readers who work in industrial settings probably have some monochronic and some polychronic traits, but are predominantly monochronic people, for that is the preponderant culture in the twenty most highly industrialized nation-states (that is, those with average yearly per capita GNPs over $15,000). (See chapter 6 for more information on the GNP of countries.)

Now that you see how perceptions of time can influence behavior, the next step is to address what you need to do differently to be effective while working with someone who perceives time differently from you.

Third, *adjust your mindset*. There are several things that David learned to do when working with Enrique. David changed his own mindset. If he was supposed to meet Enrique at a given time, he would not expect Enrique to show up until twenty to forty minutes later. In this way David would not get frustrated when Enrique didn't arrive on time. This also enabled David to plan his work schedule taking into account that Enrique would not arrive at the agreed time. On those occasions when an exact meeting time seemed necessary, David would explicitly add *hora americana* (American time) to dramatize the need for punctuality. (Stating *hora americana* [or *hora inglesa*] in contrast to *hora mexicana* is a common Mexican convention for distinguishing monochronic from polychronic time.)

---

In the next account, "silent" role definitions undermined plant productivity.

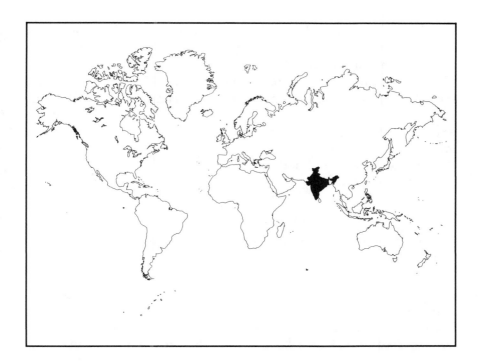

# I GET TO DECIDE *WHAT?*

An Englishwoman working in India faced some cultural values that put a few more gray hairs on her handsome head. For starters, on her first night in the country she asked for the client's help in finding suitable lodging. Given her stature and past experiences, she was visualizing well-appointed digs, perhaps a modest suite. What she found would alter forever her future expectations of hotel rooms. In its large cities, India has many hotels that would have met or exceeded Cynthia's expectations, but none of them were near this remote location. The local hotel, shabby by Western standards, was hot and muggy, and its amenities did not include a Western-style toilet, running water, or a telephone.

Cynthia's project involved working in collaboration with Indian management to raise the productivity of Mirage, Inc. To achieve the desired productivity gains, Cynthia and her U.K. team would train the first-line supervisors to make better decisions on the production floor.

The training went slower than Cynthia expected. The time lines spelled out in the original plan neglected to anticipate necessary but time-consuming rituals such as the prayer sessions that took place on company time. (Speculation circulated among the U.K. staff that the workers were praying to the Hindu God of Hope to aid the U.K. project team.) Finally, the supervisors, mostly women, were trained to make many decisions that would, in the aggregate, improve productivity.

But productivity did not improve.

## Analysis
### *What happened?*

That's the problem. The consulting team didn't have a clue to why productivity was not increasing.

### *What really happened?*

After two months of frustration, the U.K. team made an important discovery: in the Indian culture of the region, women supervisors were not expected to make the kind of important decisions that the team had trained them to make. These decisions were the prerogative of the plant manager, and his (male-dominant) culture had prepared him for this responsibility. British cultural assumptions about the role that women played in the workplace were undermining the team's progress. The women supervisors, rather than make their own decisions, continued to defer to the judgment of the plant manager. This, in effect, retained the ineffective decision-making process intact despite the training.

The belated realization by the consulting team was that the lack of gains in productivity was because the role of women supervisors precluded their doing what the U.K. team had trained them to do. This did not help the team's situation much. The client company had spent two months of high-priced fees and didn't have any results to show for them.

### *What could you do in that situation?*

An important key to avoiding belated and unpleasant news lies in the fact that it was not until the team worked side by side with the Indian supervisors that the problem came into focus.

*How can this misunderstanding be avoided in the future?*

Role expectations are a powerful shaper of behavior. It is fruitful to pay attention to whether the desired behavioral changes one expects from a training program have cultural obstacles to overcome before the changes can be comfortably implemented.

If the desired changes would be inappropriate from the trainees' perspective, it is still possible to find ways around this. Asking people who work in that setting how to do this will yield many ideas.

## INDIA, CONTINUED

Two weeks later, the plant manager left on a three-week business trip. The project team took over temporary control of the plant, and the supervisors were encouraged to make the decisions they were trained to make. Plant productivity increased fifteen percent!

The plant manager, after he returned, was faced with a dilemma: to take back the decision-making authority now delegated to the supervisors and run the risk of lowering productivity, or to maintain the new decision-making system— and the new levels of productivity. Perhaps to save face, or perhaps because he liked the new productivity levels, he decided to maintain the new system and act as though it were all part of the plan he had advocated.

The plant owners considered the consultancy a great success.

Another example of The Silent Code that governs behavior occurred in Sweden.

## NOW ABOUT THAT TALK . . .

Invited by the University of Lund to address faculty and guests on techniques for transferring educational technology to developing nations,

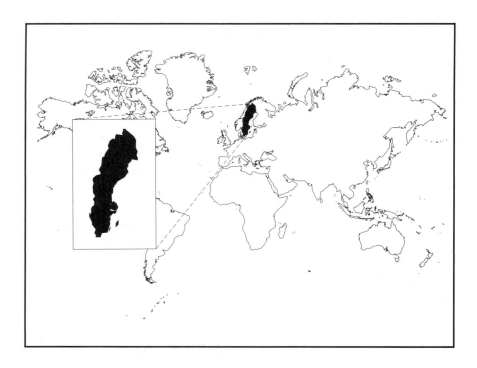

Jacqueline set about preparing the three presentations she was to make on successive days. She structured the presentations in classic U.S. style: first you tell them what you're going to tell them, then you tell them, then you tell them what you just told them. To add some spice and to provide bait for the question-answer period after the presentation, Jacqueline planned to make several provocative statements for which she refrained from providing proper foundation in the body of her address.

The talk proceeded according to plan, with one exception.

The audience did not ask any questions during the ample time Jacqueline had allotted for audience participation. As an experienced speaker, Jacqueline tried many ways to get the audience to make a comment or ask a question, but nothing she did drew a verbal response. She was unpleasantly surprised by this turn of events but did her best to hide her embarrassment.

With the empty twenty minutes still echoing in her head, Jacqueline attended other sessions where foreigners were the featured presenters. She found the same silent dynamics occurring during the question-answer period. The frustration for some of the speakers was so great they became angered at the total lack of audience response and berated them for "not getting involved."

# Analysis
## *What happened?*
Jacqueline's talk did not elicit any questions, and she was counting on questions to elaborate on several points she wanted to make.

## *What really happened?*
In this situation, the "silent code" determined the context-appropriate way to structure a talk. Violating this code caused Jacqueline some embarrassment, but a diagnosis of the problem and a prescription for improvement were close at hand (as they usually are). Once again cultural assumptions (this time on how to organize a presentation for maximum efficiency) were jeopardizing the consultant's ability to achieve results.

## *What could Jacqueline do in this situation?*
Fortunately, Jacqueline was resourceful (the hallmark of the successful consultant) and sought out a sophisticated and articulate Swede and invited her to lunch. Over smoked cod she asked her why the audience was reluctant to ask questions or make comments at the end of the presentations. "Why, that would be impolite!" her informant informed her. "That would imply that the speaker had not been clear in the presentation."

"How do Swedes organize their talks?" asked Jacqueline, sensing that all might not be well with the structured redundancy of her approach.

"Well, they present their material, then end by asking a question with a twist."

"You mean they ask a tricky question that reveals whether the speaker's main points were understood?"

"Oh, no. That would be insulting. The question is meant to suggest a possible application of the speaker's idea. A well-crafted question at the very end of a talk is very much appreciated. It leaves the listener with something to think about."

"And there is no question-answer period?" Jacqueline ventured.

"You got it."

At that point, Jacqueline restructured her remaining two talks and avoided the acute public embarrassment that had crowned her first effort.

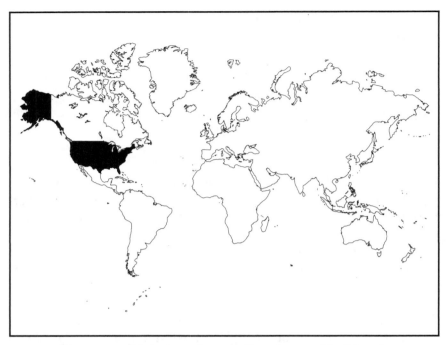

*How can this misunderstanding be avoided in the future?*

Once Jacqueline realized she had a problem, she had only to ask an informed Swede for advice. Finding the right person to ask sometimes takes a little trial and error, but you can be certain that there are people in the local culture who can articulate the cause of any misunderstanding. The initial failure might have been avoided had Jacqueline thought to ask an informed person about the lecture customs of Swedes, but hey, none of us are perfect.

---

The next example of The Silent Code illustrates yet another dimension of cultural values, how circumstances affect how one dresses.

# A SAD WOMAN'S DRESS

In one multicultural workplace in the state of Massachusetts in the eastern United States, an irrepressibly fun-loving, somewhat boisterous supervisor noticed that one of his workers, an Italian woman, appeared particularly depressed. In an attempt to get her to smile he offered her—with a theatrical flourish—a handkerchief.

"What's that for?" she asked.

"Well," the supervisor replied, smiling, "you look so sad I thought I'd offer you my handkerchief to dry your tears."

"My mother died yesterday," the grief-stricken woman said.

## Analysis
### *What happened?*
Obviously, the woman's sadness was based on heart-wrenching grief and was not tractable to kidding. But how was the foreman to know?

### *What really happened?*
The clues to her grief were there—she was dressed all in black—but the foreman missed them because in mainstream U.S. culture a black dress is more often worn for style than to signify mourning. His cultural assumptions had blocked his ability to see the signs of mourning.

### *What could the foreman do in this situation?*
The options available include sending flowers and/or a sympathy card, giving her the day off, or attending the funeral. Although in this instance the foreman did none of these, he did become immediately and seriously sympathetic. When he related this story to others in the workforce, several indicated that her black dress worn without jewelry signaled mourning.

### *How can this misunderstanding be avoided in the future?*
Awareness of this practice saved the same supervisor from blundering again when, two years later, he approached an Hispanic receptionist who was dressed all in black. Not certain of whether this was significant, the supervisor nonetheless began the conversation with unaccustomed caution. It turned out that the woman's father had died the week before—and her son had died two months before that.

---

A U.S. research team heading for Panama during a particularly volatile period was warned not to wear white shirts, especially white *guayaberas* (a popular tropical shirt worn by men outside their trousers). A dissident political group had adopted the dress as a uniform of silent protest, and the military had begun to rough up white-shirted men.

One last example of the silent code. We live in a spacy world. What with jet lag and other confusions abetted by the Age of Communications, sometimes we become a little lost in space. Let's be more concrete. How much distance do you observe between yourself and others? In Latin America, for instance, people tend to arrange themselves to be physically closer than they would in a similar situation in the United States. Ned found himself in a reception in Washington, D.C. Noticing someone he hadn't seen for several years, he joined his American colleague and his colleague's wife whom he had not met. Ned began to catch up on the news; they had many mutual friends. They began talking about friends who were living or who had lived in Latin America. Ned began to feel uncomfortable; too much distance separated them while they conversed about their friends. To close the gap, Ned stepped closer. The wife immediately stepped back the same distance. After several tries at achieving a more comfortable proximity, each time with the same unsatisfactory results, Ned began to feel irritated and judgmental. How could they have lived for so many years in Latin America without learning to get appropriately close to people while they conversed? Images of the Ugly American began to stalk Ned's good will.

It was only after the conversation that Ned remembered that the couple had not lived in Latin America—their mutual friends had. Besides, the conversation was taking place in Washington, D.C., not in Latin America. (And Ned, though Latino at heart, looks like the good Pennsylvania *gringo* he was born to be. His son, Alan—who looks generically third-world—had to remind him of this fact.) It is hard to leave behind emotional reactions to events that have been conditioned into our unconsciousness. This issue becomes particularly complex when the "outside wrapper" differs greatly from the contents inside.

## What Have We Learned from These Examples?

First, the reason that you run into "silent" problems when working in a foreign or multiculturally diverse environment stems from differences in assumptions, beliefs, and values. The more we know of our own cultural assumptions, the more aware we will be of the part these silent values play in shaping behavior. Being aware of our own silent values makes them a little less silent, a little less sneaky. People from other cultures have been socialized to internalize different values. Therefore, they react differently to many issues.

Second, there are different ways to overcome the misunderstandings that accompany conversations with people from other cultures. Some techniques used by the management consultants cited in this chapter include taking into account that time is perceived differently in different cultures and managing your expectations accordingly, and asking someone in the host country for help in interpreting the reasons for miscommunications and other workplace problems.

Before you arrive at a destination where you will be interacting with people from distinct cultures, it is cost-effective to target your reading to the country and peoples of the new assignment. The habit of doing this routinely will provide many cues to behavior that otherwise would provoke misunderstandings. Many print sources that can help us do this are listed in the bibliography at the end of the book.

Print sources are not the only way to prepare for working in another culture. Another approach is to get briefings from someone who has lived there, perhaps a native of the area. Talking with business people who have extensive experience working in a given country can give you valuable insights.

Let's return to the point that it helps if we know something about our own silent values. In addition to the silent values governing our sense of time, role expectations, appropriate dress, and how to best organize academic presentations, there are many other values that might interfere while you communicate with someone who was raised in another culture. The first step in overcoming these differences in values is to know your own silent values.

# What Are Your Cultural Assumptions?

Francis Hsu, an anthropologist, and Alfred Kraemer, a social psychologist, have identified some values which they associate with people (especially men) from mainstream U.S. society. How many of these values do you identify with? (The first four are adapted from Hsu, the remaining ones are adapted from Kraemer.)

1. An individual should believe in or acknowledge God and should belong to an organized church or other religious institution. Religion is good. Any religion is better than no religion.

2. Men and women should be treated equally.

3. Progress is good and inevitable. An individual must improve himself or herself (minimize efforts and maximize returns); the government must be more efficient to tackle new problems; institutions such as churches must modernize to make themselves more attractive.

4. Being American is synonymous with being progressive, and America is the utmost symbol of progress.

5. Each person is a distinct individual and ought to assert and achieve independence from others.

6. It is good to be action oriented ("actions speak louder than words").

7. Most interpersonal encounters serve primarily to get things done; the social significance of such encounters is secondary.

8. We tend to define other people (and even ourselves) in terms of work and achievements ("We are what we do for a living").

9. The collective wisdom of the group is superior to that of any individual ("Let's form a committee to look into that").

10. The process of decision-making requires evaluation of the consequences of alternative courses of action, and selection of the one that, on balance, seems most advantageous.

11. Competition is a good way of motivating people.

12. There is usually a best way of doing something, which should be determined and then followed.

13. Knowledge gained through observation and experience is superior to knowledge gained in other ways. (This is the view of veteran workers.)

14. Quantifying aspects of experience with numerical precision increases credibility ("We moved 1,243 desks and 2,182 chairs in seven hours and fifteen minutes today").

15. Utilitarian aspects of experience are more important than aesthetic ones.

16. We are problem solvers; there are problems in the world, and in our lives, and we should look for solutions to these problems.

17. We tend to reason in terms of probability ("There's a 65% probability of success if we follow option 3").

18. We tend to be impatient and annoyed by the slow pace of activities.

## Accepting Ourselves as Culturally Conditioned Beings

Admitting to ourselves (and to others) that we are all mightily conditioned by our cultural upbringing helps give us a handle on examining cross-cultural misunderstandings. This is harder than it seems at first. It is one thing to recognize values that are high sounding—values that any red-blooded (or blue-blooded) person would be proud to have—but it is harder to identify with values such as "Most interpersonal encounters serve primarily to get things done; the social significance of such encounters is secondary."

Whichever of the above values you have internalized into your own value system, you can be certain that many people from other cultural backgrounds have internalized quite different values. Differences in values provoke misunderstandings as we interact with host nationals.

## The Fallacy of Projected Cognitive Similarity

We are on thin ice when we attempt to interpret the behavior of others on the basis of the rationale *we* might use in similar circumstances. We may never know someone else's rationale for doing something. We cannot walk in someone else's moccasins. The psychologist Alfred Kraemer, with a playful glint reflected in his statement, calls this "The Fallacy of Projected Cognitive Similarity." Although we see the universe through our own lens, a vantage point outside the other person's value system, we can gain insight into how someone will react in certain situations.

This "fallacy" is humbling, but not devastating. "Knowledge is power [to get things done]" and the more we understand other people, the more effective we become. It's like looking through a telescope; there is more you do not see than you do, but you still see more by looking. You see even more if you remember three things:

- Time is perceived differently throughout the world.

- Manage your own expectations by revising your assumptions.

- Ask someone who knows; why did that reaction occur? How to elicit a different reaction?

| TOOLBOX |

## Checking the Silent Code

Where does the host country rank on these silent values?

**Time**  monochronic _____ polychronic
**Role of women**  subservient _____ independent
**Learning style**  lecture _____ participatory
 (memorization)  (inquiry)
**Dress**  formal _____ informal
**Body distance**
(compared to home)  close _____ distant
**Business dealings**  formal _____ informal

Generally, it is easier to learn—and employ—the silent code of the host workplace than to try to change it to be like yours. There are tricks in easing the adjustment you will be required to make:

- *Time.* Manage your expectations; don't become overly anxious.

- *Role of women.* Always treat both genders with the same respect for their intellect, stamina, and motivation. In some workplaces, relations across gender divisions need to be more formal or distant than in other settings. For example, it may not be permissible to touch a member of the opposite sex, or even make direct eye contact.

- *Learning style.* If you do not use the style the nationals are accustomed to, be sure to clearly explain what style you are using and why.

- *Dress.* Ask your counterparts about appropriate dress, and the "silent" meanings of inappropriate dress.

- *Body distance.* Ask long-term foreign residents of the host culture about this.

- *Business dealings.* Read up on this. Another source is long-term foreign business people living in the host country.

Remember:

- Some of your silent values are at best quaint and at worst upsettingly repulsive to other people.

- Don't kid yourself into thinking that you know why other people behave as they do. Just learn to anticipate how they will behave in different circumstances.

- Read up on the target culture. This will show the people you are interested in them and will give you pointers on how to get things done.

- When things go awry, ask someone who knows. This may be either a host national or a long-term foreign resident.

The examples of misunderstandings due to different cultural assumptions (time [Mexico], role [India], appropriate organization for a presentation [Sweden], the symbolic messages of dress [USA], and space [USA/Latin America]) provided in this chapter raise a question. Is there no way for international consultants to totally avoid misunderstandings? No. There is no way to avoid all misunderstandings. Just the existence of different "silent" assumptions in different people assures that we will miscommunicate to one extent or another.

With experience, we can reduce the number of misunderstandings we have with people from cultures we have "cracked," but the workplace is full of different cultures—scores of them on large international projects—and we only get to know intimately a half dozen or so. As long as we keep trotting around the globe, or as long as people from around the globe drift (or flock) into our workplace, we are destined to deal with cultural misunderstandings.

This is not as dreary a proposition as it sounds. After all, diverse perspectives can offer competitive advantages. Besides, as managers and consultants we solve workplace problems all the time.

# 4

# The Illusion of Communication

## *Understanding Cultural Contexts*

It is one thing to clear up an obvious misunderstanding, but how do you make sure that all the parties to an agreement have the same understanding when you are all sure you have understood? One key to anticipating illusionary communication is to assess the extent to which both parties' radarscopes are tuned to the same bands. Some cultures use low-context frequencies that are focused on a narrow band, while others use high-context frequencies.

## Ensuring Effective Communication

After you take your best shot at accurate communication and after everyone assumes that you were all talking about the same thing, you sometimes discover that it was all an illusion. Serious misunderstandings populate the landscape. These are generally not discovered until later, when it is costly or even impossible to renegotiate the understanding. How can these insidious misunderstandings be held in check?

In the next account, a friendly handshake contributed to a costly misunderstanding.

## WHAT HAPPENED TO THAT DECISION EVERYONE AGREED TO?

The project required accomplishing two main objectives in a factory in Oporto, a beautiful city in northern Portugal. First, installing an operator

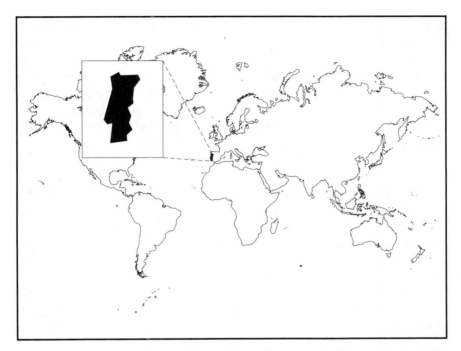

training program while training six engineers and five supervisors in manufacturing techniques; and second, modernizing twenty-two operations. Engineering the operations involved making equipment and method changes to reduce the labor content of the product so that it could be made at a lower cost. The project was scheduled for completion in four months.

The management of the client factory was a mix of Dutch and Portuguese. The Dutch plant manager spoke German and Dutch and was functional in basic Portuguese. The Portuguese production manager spoke fluent Portuguese and English, but no Dutch or German. The consulting team of five was a diverse, multilingual lot. Two of the consultants spoke Spanish, but had underestimated the extent of the differences between spoken Portuguese and Spanish. It took them a few weeks just to become accustomed to the overall rhythm of spoken Portuguese. It was a month before they could express themselves in rudimentary Portuguese.

It is not surprising, then, that with this large mix of languages and cultures, and the lack of a common language, much of the consultants' time was destined to be spent trying to communicate accurately.

The first three days on-site were consumed by planning the general strategy. Issues had to be resolved through mutual agreement. The timing of the training sessions, the scope of the training, and the personnel involved were agreed upon. At the conclusion of these initial meetings everyone shook hands, a ritual that the management consultants took to mean that both parties, the clients and the consultants, were in agreement with the contents of the sessions. Since there was no common language among those present, the meetings were conducted in a mix of several languages (Portuguese, Spanish, Dutch, and English).

The first major misunderstanding reared its ugly head on the fourth day.

Shortly after the management consulting firm's supervisors had left, the staff consultant, Alex, met with management to get the résumés of the personnel who would participate in the training. By the end of the meeting it was painfully clear that the local Portuguese management had a different interpretation of the scope of the project from that of the consultants.

The differences stemmed in part from a previous report, prepared by the consultants, that summarized the general scope of the project. What seemingly was a clear statement had been interpreted differently. It read as follows:

> Training will be given to six engineers. One of these people will also be trained as a Lead Trainer who, after the first delivery of training, will extend training to nine other persons at a second client plant in Guimaraes under the guidance of the management consultant firm.

The client had understood that the management consulting firm would extend the training to twenty-four people (fifteen technicians at the Oporto plant and nine supervisors at the Guimaraes plant); while Alex thought that his consulting company had intended to train eleven people (six supervisors and five engineers, all at the Oporto plant) and that the Portuguese lead trainer would conduct the training of the Guimaraes personnel.

Alex (who was charged with conducting the training) realized that his two supervisors (a Britisher and a Spaniard) each had a different interpretation of who would do the training and how many the training would include. Neither version coincided with that of the Portuguese management. There were five different interpretations of the contract clause!

# Analysis
## *What happened?*

The plant management and Alex had different understandings of whom he was supposed to train. He felt betrayed because the Portuguese management team had formally agreed to the contract stipulations (through formal handshakes at the end of the day.) To satisfy the client, he had to do a lot more training than he had anticipated, taking needed time from his other responsibility—modernizing almost two dozen operations.

## *What really happened?*

Even though pains had been taken to write an "unambiguous" contract clause and the message was thought by all the parties to be clear, the reality was that there were five conflicting ideas of what it said. This illusion of understanding had persisted even after three days of meetings to discuss how the project would proceed. (Incidentally, the handshakes at the close of business only signified a friendly courtesy; that is the custom in Portugal, to shake hands upon leave-taking.) What more could have been done?

## *What can Alex do now?*

The costs associated with this miscommunication were many. For one, Alex spent several days trying to clear up the confusion. This was not an easy issue to resolve: Thad had taken a vacation to sun his tired body on the white sand beaches of southern Spain and Julio was somewhere in France meeting with other clients. Second, by the time they were made fully aware one week later, Alex, under pressure from the client, had started the training course with the fifteen (rather than five) technicians. Alex soon learned that managing fifteen "foreign" technicians in a country where he had never worked before presented a respectable demand on his resources. And last, the frustration to Alex of being thousands of miles from home, in an environment where he was struggling to understand the language, had him reaching for his headache nostrums.

He did what was necessary to keep the clients happy—train whomever they wanted him to. He also had to work longer hours and request additional help from his firm.

## *How can this misunderstanding be avoided in the future?*

Cross-cultural consultants and managers inevitably find that ideas formed in the mind of the receiver differ from those of the transmitter. During

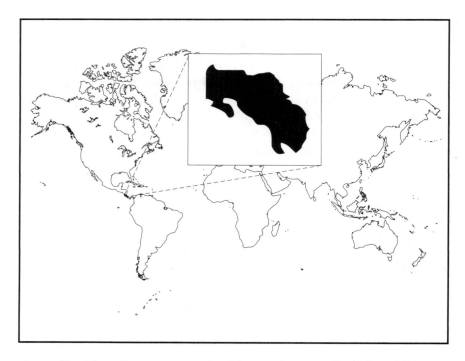

the coding/decoding process, the idea undergoes distortion. This can lead to much frustration and inefficiency on the part of both parties as demonstrated in this and the next example.

Cross-checking important points of an understanding by rewording the message in several different ways sometimes reveals misunderstandings. (The next example may give you more ideas.)

---

In the next account, factory supervisors make an unexpected error, unexpected because of the context and the redundancy of the instructions. We will re-create in some detail the context of this problem.

## HILDA'S REPAIRS

In San José, Costa Rica's capital city, a personable, easy-going bilingual engineer, Mike, worked together with Harry Whiteman, a North American plant manager who spoke limited Spanish. Their objective was to raise the productivity of the U.S.-owned plant. Mike and Harry had their work cut out for them. The plant was experiencing severe quality problems at the time and was losing considerable money.

One of the first areas where they focused their efforts was in "balancing" the plant. In industrial settings, balancing a plant means staffing all the operations so that you attain roughly the same production throughout all the operations in order to meet shipping deadlines by maintaining a low level of work-in-progress (WIP). WIP can be measured in terms of the number of weeks (or other units) of work that are in a plant. Low WIP is effective in shortening the complete business cycle—the time between the placement of the order and the delivery of the product to the customer. The reduction of WIP contributes to better customer service and lowers the actual dollars that the manufacturer has tied up in material (such as steel or fabric). Depending upon the production levels of the manufacturer, reducing WIP by one to two weeks can mean savings of more than $100,000.

Ten percent of the day was spent repairing defective garments. The current staffing was designed to produce the number of production units needed for the plant to break even and did not take into account the time spent repairing the defective garments. Consequently, the plant was not producing the necessary units.

Fortunately, Mike and Harry had the support of upper management in overcoming the losses. To alleviate the situation, they needed some information. They decided to estimate on a weekly basis how much each operator would produce in a given operation, taking into account the time lost repairing defective goods. With this information the operations could be overstaffed if necessary to meet the targets. With the cost of direct labor in this country one-sixth that of labor in the United States, this was a reasonable alternative.

If the target is to produce 1,500 units, how many trained operators would you need to achieve the target?

| Example: | without repairs | with repairs |
|---|---|---|
| Silvia | 300 | 250 |
| Cecilia | 400 | 300 |
| Miriam | 450 | 400 |
| Patricia | 350 | 325 |
| | 1,500 | 1,275 |

Using this particular work group as an example, you would need an additional worker for this group to meet its target of 1,500 units, once you take into consideration the time required for repairing defective units.

Mike explained the strategy of balancing the plant to the production manager, assistant production manager, chief industrial engineer, administrative manager, and the U.S. resident engineer. Details of the implementation were discussed. The plant manager conducted the meeting in English. Afterwards, the strategy was explained to the first-line supervisors in Spanish. Later that afternoon the plant manager, production manager, and the engineer reviewed the estimates that the supervisors had made of what each operator in their section could produce.

So far so good.

When the plant manager, production manager, and bilingual engineer reviewed the estimates individually with each supervisor, the plant manager would ask if the supervisors had taken repairs into account. They would smile and acknowledge that they had. Ana Elisa Díaz submitted a typical report.

**Ana Elisa Díaz, Supervisor**
(estimate with repairs)

| | |
|---|---|
| Hilda | 300 |
| Lucinda | 400 |
| Carmen | 200 |
| Raquel | 100 |
| Roxinia | 500 |
| | 1,500 |

Mike knew the operators well by then and realized that Ana Elisa had overestimated their production.

To double-check this, Mike asked the supervisor a few more direct questions in Spanish. "How much can Hilda produce if she does not have to do repairs?" "How many repairs does she normally do in a day?" "How long does it take her to repair these defective garments?" "How many pieces can she produce in a day, assuming she will have to do repairs?"

The responses to these questions prompted new estimates that demonstrated that the operation needed another operator to reach the 1,500 units/day level.

**Estimates with time for repairs considered**

| | |
|---|---|
| Hilda | 250 |
| Lucinda | 375 |
| Carmen | 175 |
| Raquel | 100 |
| Roxinia | 450 |
| Another operator | 150 |
| | 1,500 |

Out of this review Mike found that the production manager had understood that the estimates were not to take into account time spent on repairs. Why hadn't she understood that the reverse was true?

# Analysis
## *What happened?*
The general manager discussed the plan directly with his five middle managers: administration manager, quality manager, chief industrial engineer (IE), U.S. resident engineer, and production manager. Of the five middle managers, the production manager had to explain the program to the supervisors who would ultimately implement the plan.

The production manager did not take into consideration the time the operators spent doing repairs when she calculated the staffing needed to meet production quotas. This in spite of "clear" directions to the contrary. She also did not communicate the proper sense of urgency to the supervisors when she explained what they were to do.

## *What really happened?*
The "clear" directions on how to calculate staffing patterns were not understood (if they were heard at all) by the production manager. The problem stemmed from Mike and Harry ignoring the key role of the production manager when they explained the task to her along with the

assistant production manager, chief IE, and administrative manager. It was imperative for her to have a precise understanding of the task, and this was not adequately assured.

### What can Mike do now?

He did what he should have done: he diplomatically asked questions to help the production manager clear up the error in calculation.

### How can this misunderstanding be avoided in the future?

For an organization to function effectively it must be able to communicate clearly. This example demonstrates that when a message is not clearly conveyed, it can result in acute financial losses. The cost of these losses in this case were aggravated by the company-wide implications of the program that was being implemented. In this case, if the program were not implemented properly, the shipping deadlines could not be met.

A number of factors led to this misunderstanding. First, the strategy was explained in English and although it appeared (through nonverbal signs) that the production manager had understood, she had not. She had a reasonable understanding of English, so she may possibly have believed she understood the strategy, or perhaps she did not want to admit that it was not clear how it would work in order to save face in front of her peers and subordinates. Or maybe her mind had wandered at a critical point in the discussion. Although a handout was distributed with concrete examples, she may not have taken the time to read through how the procedure would work.

Even though great efforts were made to ensure a clear understanding of the implementation process, the key person in making it happen had not understood. Mike was able to help the team overcome the miscommunication by following up on the actual implementation of the plan. Mike's awareness of the productivity levels of individual operators prompted him to suggest that he and Harry go around with the production manager to review the estimates with the individual supervisors. Through this effort the plant was able to avoid further late shipments, keeping the customers satisfied. Moral of the story: Ya gotta stay close to the data source to avoid GIGO (garbage in, garbage out).

A story from a project in the Caribbean will illustrate another type of miscommunication provoked by language barriers.

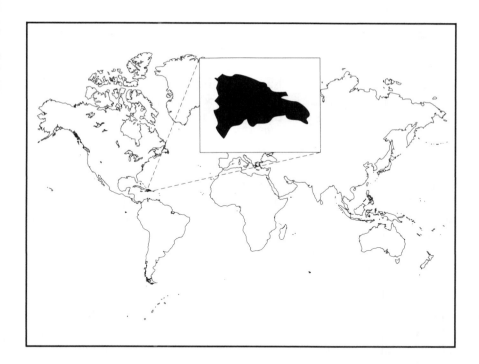

## "ALMOST" GETTING THE POINT

Throughout the soft goods chain, the effort to bring costs down and to provide better customer service is putting new demands on the links of the chain. Customers are now demanding many more styles in smaller quantities. These changes are causing retailers to buy merchandise differently from their past practices. To meet these new customer demands, manufacturers must be able to respond quickly. This means shortening the lead time, the time from when an order arrives at the receiving dock until it is shipped from the plant.

There are techniques to do this.

In a meeting in the Dominican Republic, Johnny Walker, the Vice President of a U.S. pants manufacturer; Oscar, the local plant manager; and Bud and Lou, two members of a management consulting group, discussed the details of changing the factory's work system from progressive bundle unit (PBU) lines to modules in response to pressure from retailers to improve customer service. It is not uncommon for modular installations to succeed in reducing lead time from ten days (in the traditional system) to two days.

The difference between PBU lines and a modular approach is this. In traditional sewing lines, operators sew a bundle (a variable number of garments) and then pass the bundles to the subsequent operations, whose operators do the same. The incentive to an individual worker lies in production. The more they produce, the more they earn. In a modular system a group of operators works together to manufacture a product. This self-managing group checks each other's quality at every operation; the incentive paid to each operator in the module depends upon how the module performs as a whole. The benefits of working in modules include lower carrying costs, lower work-in-progress (WIP), improved quality, and quicker throughput time.

During the meeting, Oscar, the hard-working Dominican plant manager, interrupted the meeting to ask a question concerning the new incentive plan that was to be implemented to motivate the operators during the changeover from traditional lines to modules. Johnny, the U.S. V.P., responded and the ensuing discussion took place half in English and half in Spanish, as both spoke their second language haltingly.

"How you want to pay the operators when are in the modules?" asked the Dominican plant manager.

"Let's pay them at their average for the first four weeks in the module," said the U.S. V.P.

"So, the group paid at average?" Oscar verified.

"Yes, their four-week average," responded Johnny.

At the end of the discussion they both smiled. It became apparent to one of the consultants, Lou, however, that they had not agreed on the same incentive plan. Oscar had understood that each week the operators would be paid according to the average weekly performance of the module. Johnny meant that for the first four weeks each operator would be paid at his or her previous four-week average, after which the pay would depend on the performance of the module as a whole.

During the first weeks after inception, the performance of the module would be poor, as it always is at first when a work team changes its modus operandi. The incentive plan that Oscar understood would have taken away the incentive to produce—the module operator would have been discouraged after receiving low pay because the module's performance was low. What Johnny had described was designed to protect the earnings of the operators while they adjusted to working in a modular system. Since their earnings were protected, they wouldn't become overly frustrated during the trying initial weeks.

The plant manager planned to explain the new incentive scheme to the engineers, module members, and payroll. Luckily, the difference was clarified before the module started down a dead-end street.

# Analysis
### What happened?
The V.P. explained a new incentive plan to the plant manager, and both agreed that it would be a good idea.

### What really happened?
The plant manager misunderstood how the worker incentives were to be calculated.

### What can be done now?
This misunderstanding was only momentary because they had the good fortune to have someone present during the discussion who was fluent in both Spanish and English. One cannot always rely on good fortune.

### How can this misunderstanding be avoided in the future?
This misunderstanding again illustrates an environment ripe for misunderstanding and how important it is to check or cross-validate one's understanding of an agreement. A chart graphing the training curve may have aided.

Boye De Mente, in his book on doing business in Korea, illustrates a problem stemming from ambiguity. If you say, "Don't you know his phone number?," the answer you receive may be "Yes," meaning "Yes, you are right. I don't know his phone number." This can cause confusion and frustration and can be avoided by phrasing all questions in the positive form.

Often, the international manager or consultant deals with people who are fluent in the shared language. In this next example, the common language is English.

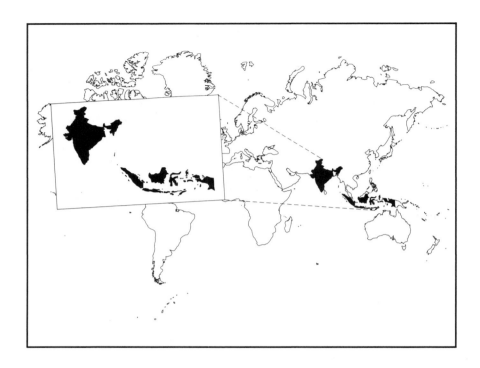

# ONE TONGUE IS NOT ENOUGH!

The U.S. Agency for International Development wanted to know whether it was feasible to measure the effectiveness of an educational innovation that many countries are developing in an effort to extend educational opportunity to more of their citizens. The innovation, bilingual education, allows children to understand the teacher in their own language. "Monolingual" countries typically insist on teaching children in the "official" language, rather than in the language they speak at home, in an attempt to forge a national citizenry with whom government can communicate efficiently. This was especially true of colonial governments. It is not at all unusual for a country to have hundreds of different languages spoken within its borders.

The objective of the study was to determine whether it was technically viable to compare the achievement of educational programs taught in so many distinct languages and under varying social and economic conditions. Were government officials willing to participate in an international evaluation? And if so, under what conditions? These were the questions that needed to be answered.

Hugh, an educational evaluator, was contracted to visit various South and Southeast Asian countries to assess the feasibility of this cross-national evaluation. He selected countries where he knew bilingual education was available to at least some children. He began in India, a country which at that time had fourteen "official" languages (languages that can be used to conduct governmental affairs) and 500 additional languages. After setting up an appointment with the proper educational specialists in the Department of Education in New Delhi, Hugh stated the purpose of his visit.

"I'm interested in gaining an overview of bilingual education in India."

"There is no bilingual education in India," the education official replied.

"There's no bilingual education anywhere in the country?" responded a perplexed Hugh.

"No, nowhere."

The interview was off to an inauspicious start.

Hugh pressed on. "You mean there is no school where children are taught in their home language while at the same time taught a second language?"

"Oh yes, many such schools," came the reply.

"Then why do you say that you don't have any examples of bilingual education?"

"Because it is *trilingual* education. The children in those schools learn Hindi and English as second and third languages."

At this point, the interview became productive.

Hugh's next stop was the city-state of Singapore, where he attended a week's conference on language use in elementary schools in Southeast Asia. One two-day segment he attended dealt with Singapore schools in which there were large numbers of native speakers of diverse languages. In designated schools, children were taught through the medium of English or Chinese or Tamil or Malaysian.

The presenters used a common linguistic convention to describe the schools. "L1" referred to the "first language," "L2" to the second language, and "L3" to the third language. In some schools the L1 was Chinese; in others, English. And so on. They would say things such as

"Students who go to these L1 Chinese schools learn English as L2," which Hugh took to mean that Chinese students went to certain schools and were taught English as a second language.

But sometimes Hugh could make no sense of what the presenters were saying. For example, "These Chinese students go to an L1 English school where they learn Tamil as L2." If the students' L1 was Chinese, how could they go to an English-language school and learn English as L1? And wouldn't Tamil be L3 in this case, rather than L2?

It took a whole day before Hugh realized that the L1, L2, L3 descriptors did not refer to the students' home languages, but to the language of instruction used in the schools. If Chinese students went to an L1 English school, they were taught in English and learned Tamil as their third language (the L2 or L3 of the school).

The next stop was Indonesia. Hugh told the Department of Education officials that he was interested in bilingual schools. "Or trilingual," he added. An obviously concerned, perhaps even upset, official responded, "Bilingual education is against the law in Indonesia."

Hugh described the classroom situation that, for Hugh, implied bilingual education. Namely, that the student was being taught subject matter areas in his or her home language, while learning the national language, Bahasa Indonesia, as a second language.

"Oh," said the official, "there are several exceptions to the law in cases where the local culture has a long and illustrious literary history. In those cases, we provide *vernacular language education* in the early grades."

It turned out there were nine such language areas, such as Balinese and Javanese.

## Analysis
### *What happened?*
The focus of Hugh's study—bilingual education—turned out to be particularly susceptible to misunderstanding in an international context.

### *What really happened?*
Terms that are deeply rooted in one cultural setting translate only roughly into languages in which experience with the terms has been molded by different historical antecedents. Words such as *democracy*, *crime*, *freedom*, *education*, *home*, *buildings*, *appropriate dress*, *etiquette*, and

*respect*, clearly fall into this category. How might an Eskimo visualize the concept of table etiquette? The Queen of England? The Flintstones? Cultures develop vocabularies and nonverbal structures based on their needs and experiences. Terminology is only directly translatable when the sender and receiver share the same understanding of what the word means. (An example of a word that has a different meaning in another culture is the word *snow*—some Eskimo languages have hundreds of different words to identify it, depending on the type of snow, when and where it fell, and so on.) Hugh erroneously assumed that *bilingual education*, a term used in the United States (and some other countries as well), would convey about the same meaning to educators in Southeast Asia.

### *What can Hugh do now?*

When Hugh abandoned the term *bilingual education* in favor of an operational description of the school setting he was seeking, the problem disappeared.

### *How can this misunderstanding be avoided in the future?*

Be wary of the images that words in one language conjure in the minds of speakers of other languages. What implications does this have for the cross-cultural manager? A tool to help avoid misinterpretations is to explain critical terms and verify understanding throughout the conversation by rewording the presumed understanding.

For the rest of his trip, Hugh stopped calling the object of his study "bilingual education." Instead, he described the classroom situation he was seeking in behavioral terms.

---

In the previous examples, we saw four points at which cross-cultural communication often breaks down. Namely, when the manager or consultant does not speak the host language, when he speaks it but not quite well enough, when nonverbal signs (for example, shaking hands) carry messages that are important to a supposed agreement, and when the same term exists in both cultures but with markedly different meanings.

Accurate communication is a vital prerequisite to effective management in any setting in which one is trying to increase the efficiency of the client organization. Whether you are implementing a training program in Mexico or trying to raise the productivity of an apparel plant in Portugal, your ability to communicate clearly, as well as your ability to understand others, will be a key factor in achieving results at the lowest economical, political, social, and cultural cost.

What are the costs of miscommunication?

- Frustration and resentment spent clearing up misunderstandings.

- Backtracking when you discover everyone did not in fact "agree" to the same decision.

- Potential loss of profitable deals.

- Lessened ability to sell, negotiate, persuade, implement, give directions, and motivate.

- Decisions based on misinformation.

Even knowing the critical areas where cross-cultural communication breaks down, how can we avoid misunderstandings? In all of the above examples, the participants thought they understood. But this was an illusion. They did not realize that there were critical differences in how they and their partners understood key issues.

One useful intercultural skill is that of recognizing the symptoms of cultural misunderstanding when they do appear.

---

| TOOLBOX |

# Recognizing the Symptoms of Misunderstandings

Signs for recognizing when you encounter cultural misunderstandings:

- blank stares

- unnatural stopping points in conversation

- embarrassment in the other person

- non sequiturs

- feelings of "not connecting"

What to do?

- Stop and do a reality check. Try to figure out why you aren't connecting.

- If the point seems important, invite someone to interpret. (As the Portugal example demonstrates, there will be times when even after watching for verbal and nonverbal cues there is still miscommunication.)

- If the point does not seem immediately critical or if you don't want to interrupt the conversation, make a note of the occurrence and ask someone about it later.

There are certain basic tools that can facilitate the communication process when working in a multicultural context: conversing tools, language training, and working with translators.

| TOOLBOX |

# Converting Communicative Illusion into Reality

- Cross-check important points by rewording the message in different ways to surface any misunderstandings. (Open-ended questions, repetition, and paraphrasing are particularly advisable in situations where there is a high risk of misunderstanding. Meetings in which several languages are being spoken are prime examples of "high-risk" situations.)

- Use visual aids and numbers whenever possible to convey key points. (Remember what Confucius said about one picture.)

- Check the buzz words that are repeated often in the conversation to see if they are being used in the same way by your partner. Avoid the use of idiomatic expressions and slang. Evaluate the meaning and cultural connotations of the key labels to be used in training, plant management, or product identification.

- Ascertain (preferably before your conversation) the real meaning of nods and verbal assents. They do not always mean agreement.

(In Japan, *hai* [yes] means "Yes, I hear what you're saying." It does not mean "Yes, I agree with what you're saying.")

- Hold off deciding what the other person is saying until you get the whole message, or at least a larger chunk of it. Then ask questions to check your understanding.

- Keep good notes.

- Follow up after you have begun to implement an agreement to confirm the understanding.

The next chapter discusses the implication of working in corporate settings in which the cognitive style differs significantly from your own, including the differences between high- and low-context cultures.

When the manager or consultant is from a low-context culture in which much of the message is in the words, he or she may need more help while working in high-context countries, where much more of the nonverbal context is relevant to "the real meaning," to "hidden" messages. Conversely, when a high-context individual works in a low-context culture, he or she may need more help in focusing on the relevant issues: things may be *less* than they seem. You can get this help from your supervisors or from local people who understand both cultures.

# 5

# In at the Deep End
## Developing Rapport in the Multicultural Workplace

This chapter examines three culturally general issues critical to developing rapport in the multicultural workplace. What guidelines will help establish rapport when you interact with a culture you know little about? How do you manage your own and your hosts' sense of ethnocentrism? How do you establish bona fides, a critical prerequisite to developing rapport in most settings?

## Following General Guidelines

Alas, this is not the best of all possible worlds.

The next story illustrates one of the realities of much intercultural sojourning—finding yourself in a situation you are unprepared to handle. It could happen in a multicultural workplace at home or on an overseas assignment.

## COMING, READY OR NOT

Let's say your boss calls you to his office one afternoon and asks you if you are doing anything important. He then describes a problem in one of the branch offices, tells you that you have three weeks to resolve it, hands you a plane ticket, and wishes you *bon voyage*. "Try to finish up the stuff you're working on by the end of the week," your boss adds. Since it is Friday, you assume that means the boss expects you to work

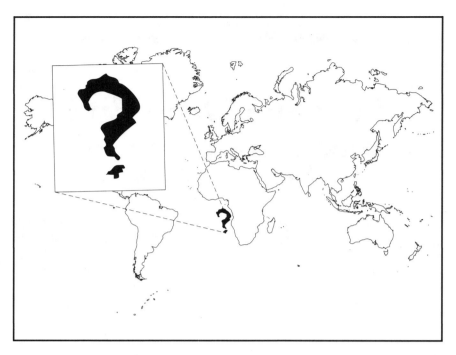

on Saturday and Sunday. You nervously open the ticket and discover your flight leaves Tuesday morning. Worse! It's for an overseas country you have difficulty pronouncing. You vaguely remember having seen it once on a map but don't remember the continent. And that's about all you know about it. (This is a true story.)

## Analysis
### *What happened?*
You are being sent to a country you know little or nothing about.

### *What really happened?*
Nothing very unusual. International managers and consultants often are sent to countries they have not visited before.

### *What can you do now?*
No matter how internationally experienced we are, we move in and out of cultures that are new to us. We find ourselves in countries we have never visited, and we work with colleagues from cultures we know little

about. What are we to do to improve the quality of these transitions into the unknown? Because you don't have time to read up on the target country—much less learn a handful of phrases in the language—you will have to rely on *general* guidelines for effective interpersonal behavior that usually prove effective in intercultural consulting. What help (help!) can we offer to the hapless international consultant who wants to avoid falling flat on his or her face right off the plane but who knows nothing about the local customs? What are the *general* guidelines for ingratiating yourself in a strange culture?

## Which Guidelines Will Help?

Once you have devised a strategy for communicating effectively, you find yourself communicating with flesh-and-blood people—individuals all, each with his or her own style and worldview. The name of the game becomes making—and keeping—good relationships.

An insight into what culturally naive people think helps grease the wheels of intercultural communication is provided by Judith Martin and Mitch Hammer who report on a survey of white undergraduate students enrolled in speech communication courses in a U.S. Midwestern university. The 602 respondents had not traveled much outside the United States. They were asked what they considered to be the behaviors associated with competence in both intracultural and intercultural communication. (Since the respondents had little international experience and probably had little domestic intercultural experience as well, they gave similar responses to both research categories.) The most common behaviors listed were, in order of popularity: show interest in the other, in what they say (54%); listen carefully (46%); maintain direct eye contact (39%); smile (36%); ask questions about the other person (34%); ask questions about the other's country (28%); be friendly (28%); ask questions (24%); share information about self (24%); speak clearly (18%); seek topics of mutual interest (17%).

University students in other countries can be expected to propose different facilitating behaviors. Even different ethnicities within the United States may assign different priorities to the list of behaviors they feel may facilitate intercultural communication. Mexican American students, according to Hecht, Ribeau, and Sedano, rate very highly eye contact that conveys agreement. One suspects that this may be more important to many Latin Americans than smiling; they are not dazzled by your smile so much as by that sparkle in your eyes. The important ways to establish rapport depend on whom you ask.

Is that it? Listen, ask questions, smile and sparkle? No, we can be more helpful. Daniel J. Kealey of the Canadian International Development Agency offers a particularly interesting sketch of effective technical advisers who work overseas. Their seven key characteristics emerged from ratings by peers and researchers. According to this study, effective technical advisers exhibit the following behaviors:

1. Demonstrate *caring* behavior as indicated by:
   - the capacity to build and maintain friendly, cooperative, trusting relationships with others
   - the capacity to show interest in, attentiveness to, and respect for others
   - sensitivity to local realities, social, political, and cultural
   - empathy, the ability to read suffering or discomfort on another person's face. A sense of competence in perceiving the needs and feelings of others.

2. Demonstrate *action-orientation* as indicated by:
   - initiative, being one of the first to act, making suggestions, proposing a plan of action
   - self-confidence, expressing and demonstrating self-confidence with regard to personal goals and judgment
   - frankness, being frank and open in dealing with others

3. Demonstrate *"out-of-self orientation"* as indicated by:
   - control, being calm and in control when confronted by interpersonal conflict or stress
   - flexibility and being open to new ideas, other beliefs, and the points of view of others
   - perseverance, when tasks become overly frustrating, persisting in working toward the goals
   - teamwork, preferring to work with others rather than alone

4. Demonstrate *low need for upward mobility* as indicated by:
   - de-emphasis on the need for high earnings
   - de-emphasis on the need to live in a desirable area
   - de-emphasis on the need for advancement
   - de-emphasis on the need to work in a prestigious company

5. Demonstrate *low security needs* as indicated by:
   - not [unduly] being worried by tension and job stress
   - not needing good physical working conditions
   - not needing security of employment
   - not needing your boss's OK for everything you do
   - not needing a well-defined job situation

6. Demonstrate *high self-monitoring* as indicated by:
   - skill at reading social situations
   - skill at regulating personal behavior to meet the needs of the situation

7. Demonstrate *social adroitness* as indicated by:
   - skill at persuading others to achieve certain goals
   - being diplomatic
   - social intelligence

These seven interaction styles are worth cultivating. Some of them, of course, depend on knowing details of the host culture that first-time sojourners rarely possess. For example, "respect for others" requires knowing how respect is demonstrated in the host culture. But for the most part, these styles do not require a deep understanding of the host culture. Had one U.S. manager working in Nigeria understood Kealey's point about de-emphasizing the need for high earnings, he might have fared better (see "A Cost-Effective Request," page 74).

# How Can You Avoid Being Sent to Places You Know Nothing About?

Ha! You are a real dreamer if you think you will always have the information you need prior to arrival in a strange land. Fortunately, there are ways to predict how to go about building relationships in a society you know little about.

The more we know about a given society, the more we can hypothesize behaviors that will make our boundary crossings easier on all involved. Many of the behaviors that will reduce the strain on host nationals as they interact with us may be predictable from a knowledge of larger cultural themes or theoretical constructs, of which there are about thirty in current use in intercultural research. Whichever theoretical construct you use, you are able to predict a certain amount of behavior. Some constructs are more useful than others for hypothesizing behavior in certain specific domains (for example, economic, political, or social).

For our purposes, let us picture a continuum of critical behaviors. That is, behaviors that contribute directly to successful interaction with host-culture people, and which, in their absence, most probably will provoke friction.

### Behavior Critical to Acceptance

| culturally general | culture-class general | culturally specific |
|---|---|---|

On the left-hand extreme are ingratiating culturally general behaviors that guests usually can perform without any knowledge of the specific culture. Kealey's seven suggestions fall into this category. To the right of the culturally general end of the continuum are behaviors that are typical of a *class* of cultures (that is, cultures with significantly shared traits, such as among Hispanic cultures or among Arab cultures). These behaviors can be predicted from the very modest knowledge base that a successful theoretical model requires; they are the subject of the next chapter. Marking the right-hand end of the continuum—the longest part—are the many culture-specific behaviors that cannot be effectively predicted without precise knowledge of a particular culture. This latter type consists of the many principles and discrete behaviors that an average person socialized in the host culture would possess but which a cultural outsider—even an armchair expert on the country—may not know. These are dealt with in chapter 7.

## Which Models of Culture Are Most Useful?

Now let us concentrate on the extreme left-hand side of our continuum of critical behaviors, on those that are common to most cultures.

Even single-trait models can be useful as you seek to build relationships, for sometimes a single variable contains powerful predictive ability. A single-trait construct can ask whether or not the trait is present, or it can ask to what extent the trait is present.

An example of the it's-either-there-or-not approach is elaborated by Gerhard and Jean Lenski in their text, *Human Societies: An Introduction to Macrosociology.* The Lenskis identify basic food-providing technologies (for example, hunting and gathering, horticulture [wooden digging poles], agriculture [metal-tipped plows], industrialization) and identify beliefs and behaviors typical of each. The trait (that is, the type of food-gathering technology employed), once identified, predicts a long list of behaviors. Knowing that a society obtains its food from agriculture, for instance, enables you to hypothesize that there will be widely varying social and economic levels, from the wealthiest to the most impoverished. In fact, the most highly stratified societies in human history have been agrarian. In these societies, the international consultant will want to give proper deference to the hierarchical nature of the workplace and society in general. Knowing that a society obtains its food mostly from hunting and gathering, on the other hand, allows you to hypothesize that that society will observe few social class distinctions, and that the difference between the wealthiest and poorest members will be relatively slight. This macrosociological approach implies that it is the technology that causes the behavior.

An example of the to-what-extent-is-the-trait-present approach is asking what the average per capita gross national product (GNP) is for a given country. Knowing that the society has a low per capita GNP, you can predict that people will expect the government, rather than private enterprise, to shoulder the major responsibility for improvement in the quality of life. Further, you can predict that the mass media will be controlled by the state and that there will be a drastic difference in the lifestyles of rural and urban peoples (paucity of electricity, medical assistance, markets in rural areas). And so on.

The next account illustrates the violation of a very common convention, especially in less-developed nations. Unfortunately, it is one whose observation is critical to making a favorable impression in a new culture. The desired behavior accords deference to host-national ethnocentrism.

---

# HERE'S HOW WE DO IT BACK
# WHERE I'M FROM

---

The project was a five-year effort to raise the awareness of the population to issues affecting good health. Pamphlets on hygiene, construction of

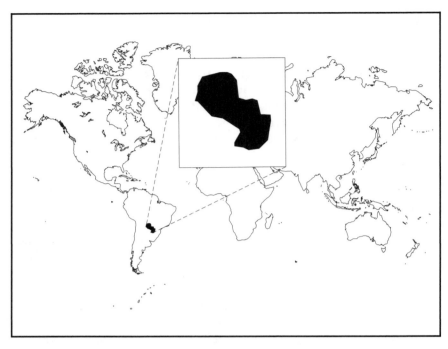

latrines, preparation of food, birthing, and other similar topics were to be prepared. The technical adviser for the project was an American who was fluent in Spanish, Dr. Robert Fuentes (not his real name). The twenty people who comprised the five-person teams to produce the health materials had not had previous experience in writing and publishing educational pamphlets. They had worked as paraprofessional "health promoters" in villages before assignment to this national project. Dr. Fuentes tried to provide them with general administrative guidelines for writing and producing the pamphlets. To this end, he would assemble the teams together at regular intervals and give them carefully prepared lectures on various aspects of the project. Eventually it became clear that the team members were still confused about what they had to do to produce effective materials. Dr. Fuentes then began sending the project supervisors detailed generic outlines of the proposed pamphlets, along with specific examples of similar health education materials that had been prepared in the United States for rural Spanish-speaking areas such as the Southwestern United States.

He would often punctuate his advice with remarks such as, "In

America we . . ." or "These materials proved very effective in those parts of the United States where we had similar circumstances." The supervisors and team members listened respectfully but did not adopt Dr. Fuentes' suggestions. In time, some negative feedback reached his ears. The team members did not think the United States had similar circumstances to those of Paraguay, and they did not see the relevance of U.S. materials to their problems.

Dr. Fuentes then began looking for curriculum materials in other Latin American countries. A project in Costa Rica looked especially promising, as did one in Mexico and another in Argentina. It took considerable effort to assemble these materials, and he made a presentation to the whole group extolling their relevance and inviting the team members to drop by his office on the first floor to examine them. Still, the Paraguayan team did not adopt any of the materials. In fact, it was hard to find any evidence that they had even looked at these materials.

By the third year of the project, two things were painfully clear: the team was doing a very poor job of materials preparation (they were two years behind schedule), and the team ignored virtually all of Dr. Fuentes' suggestions.

## Analysis
### *What happened?*
Dr. Fuentes' ideas were not accepted. Were they impractical or out of place?

### *What really happened?*
Dr. Fuentes' use of the United States as a frame of reference assured that whatever idea he advanced was not going to get much of a hearing. (And he called it "America," which additionally alienated the proud Paraguayans—after all, Paraguay is in America, too.) Even when he switched to examples from other parts of Latin America, he got the same reaction: Paraguay was unique; materials from other countries could not be appropriate.

It is common practice for cultures to attempt to establish their uniqueness (and often superiority) by proving other cultures different (and often inferior). The actions of "outsiders" are looked upon with irrelevance or contempt. William Graham Sumner, in his classic study, called this view of one's group as the center of everything "ethnocentrism." Levine and Campbell, in their exhaustive review of the dynamics of ethnocentrism, contrast attitudes and behaviors of the in-group toward those of the out-group.

The in-group:

1. See themselves as virtuous and superior

2. See their own standards of value as universal and intrinsically true

3. See themselves as strong

4. Strive for cooperative relations with in-group members

5. Are obedient to in-group authorities

6. Are willing to remain an in-group member

The in-group's view of the out-group:

1. See the out-group as contemptible, immoral, and inferior

2. See the out-group as weak

3. Do not strive to cooperate with out-group members

4. Are not obedient to out-group authorities

5. Do not want to convert to out-group membership

6. Use out-groups as bad examples in the training of children

7. Blame the out-group for the in-group's troubles

8. Distrust the out-group

Ethnocentrism is related to "phenomenal absolutism," the tendency to assume that the world is exactly as one sees it, and that all other persons, groups, or cultures perceive the world in the same way, but behave differently out of a perverse wickedness or incompetence.

An overdose of ethnocentrism can manifest itself as xenophobia, a strong dislike or distrust of foreigners, and may lead to isolationism. By using the "ostrich defense," xenophobic societies try to avoid contact with differing cultures to keep themselves from being infected by foreign cultures. Censorship of the media is one way to keep people thinking "decent" thoughts.

### *What can Dr. Fuentes do now?*

Unfortunately, Dr. Fuentes had isolated himself from people who might have aided him. His office was on a different floor, and he chose to work on a face-to-face basis exclusively with a few high-ranking administrators. He would lecture to supervisors and the rest of the workforce in large groups. He never rolled up his sleeves to work side by side with those who were producing what he lectured about. These behaviors were regarded by host nationals as part and parcel of the "outsider" status of Dr. Fuentes. After working in this environment for three years, he left with only token displays of interpersonal warmth. He did not achieve any substantial project objectives.

### *How can this misunderstanding be avoided in the future?*

Don't try to convince people of a new way to do something by saying "In X [usually a high-status] country they do. . . ." In most countries of the world, people think of themselves and their country as unique, even when a demographer would see few salient differences. What works in another country, people reason, cannot work here because we are so different, so special.

---

# Ethnocentrism vs. Cultural Relativism

A few years ago, the authors studied Japanese quality control groups in more than 700 U.S. companies (where the preferred term was *quality circles*). Quality circles are composed of six to a dozen or so employees who work together making gizmos or providing a service. This group of work cohorts proposes changes in the way they operate—sometimes drastic changes costing management sizable amounts of money (but holding the carrot of greater cost savings). They research alternative ways, present their findings to upper management, and show why the proposed changes will increase company productivity or the quality of life. These participative management groups have saved billions of dollars in Japanese companies. The underlying philosophy is that operational changes are best proposed by those most closely associated with the problem, regardless of their job titles.

The authors encountered some resistance on the part of many U.S. managers to adopt quality circles. "They may work in Japan," we were told, "but this is the U.S. We have a different culture here." This criticism was doubly ironic. The idea for quality circles did not originate with the Japanese: it came from two U.S. management consultants, W. Edwards Deming and Joseph M. Juran, who could not get U.S. industry heads to listen to them. Japanese corporate leaders did. The double irony? First, why did the American ideas work in Japan? Second, why wouldn't American ideas work in the U.S.? Still, it's a knee-jerk reaction to reject "foreign" ideas.

As we discussed in the first section of this book, your cultural upbringing determines how you see the world, and it does not take a rocket scientist to predict that you see your culture as morally superior to most others—if not to *all* others. It is a universal of human behavior: everyone is taught to be ethnocentric.

Through our upbringing we learn to value certain traits. This is important to our survival and contribution as a productive member of society. These traits serve as our personal guide. When an individual crosses into another culture, differences in cultural values present a sticky wicket for the international consultant to negotiate. An important culturally general skill that will enhance effective intercultural relations is to keep a firm hold on the reigns of your own ethnocentrism.

"Cultural relativism" is the opposite of ethnocentrism. The cultural relativism school rejects the ethnocentric mode of judging other cultures. It denies the validity of any one standard for evaluating cultural phenomena. Relativists believe that a culture can only be assessed in terms of its geographical, historical, and social context. To do otherwise would be to judge soccer by the rules of tennis.

These cultural attitudes will influence our ability to establish a working relationship with someone from another culture. Needless to say, strongly ethnocentric people will find their attitude unwelcome in the international arena.

An exceptionally important directive: work alongside your counterparts, helping to resolve problems; avoid dictating to them.

The next vignette will illustrate another important dynamic that is often a prerequisite to establishing rapport in the workplace, especially for itinerant here-today-gone-tomorrow consultants.

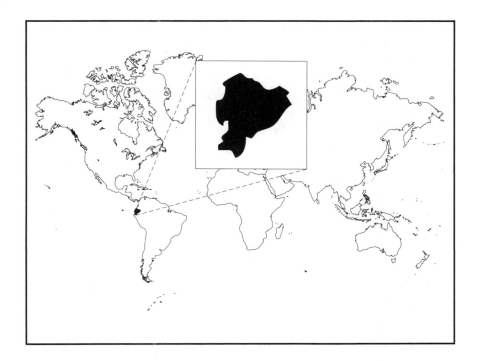

# KEEPING YOUR HEAD DURING
# INTRODUCTIONS

Gathering baseline data is always fraught with difficulties. Ned was assigned to gather community information that would be relevant to the improvement of an innovative education program. They say the devil is in the details. The communities in question were Shuar, seminomadic hunters and gatherers living in eastern Ecuador in the upper-Amazon basin. They were reachable by dugout canoes (this would take a week or two to reach each village) or by light airplane seating three passengers. Since time was a factor, arrangements were made for Ned and three companions who spoke Spanish and Shuar to be flown to each village. Or rather, to be flown kind of *close* to the villages to be sampled. (The Shuar, incidentally, had been the recipients of considerable international notoriety due to the unique artifacts they had produced up to several years before the author's survey—shrunken heads.)

The interviewers arrived, survey forms in hand, at the tiny airstrip about mid-afternoon after an hour's flight. The pilot promptly informed the group that he was heading out—at his own expense—and would return in two days to pick them up.

"Why not stay in the village with the rest of us?" Ned asked.

"Because of the bats. This village has a bad reputation."

"Bats?"

"Yeah, vampire bats." With that exchange, the pilot revved up the motor and was gone.

Ned looked at his teammates, and they shrugged their shoulders. "The malaria mosquitoes are really of more concern," they said.

The trek from the airstrip to the village was worthy of the most intrepid jungle explorer.

It was dusk when the last member of the team arrived at the village of a half dozen pole-and-thatched homes. Most of the villagers liked to keep a couple of kilometers between themselves and their nearest neighbors, so it took some time for the villagers to assemble. The team stood on the elevated porch of the tiny school while the villagers trickled in. Nobody said anything; all waited for the village leader and spokesperson to arrive. When he did, he did not exude cheerfulness. In a stern, disapproving tone of voice that matched his face, he looked at the research team and pointed to each in turn.

"I know who you are," he said to the interviewer who lived in the village. "And I know who you are," he said to the second team member, someone who had some years before lived in the community. "And I know who you are," he said (more like shouted) to the third member of the team, a Shuar who lived in a neighboring village. Then facing Ned, he said, "Who are you?" The tone was not friendly. Ned did not have to understand much Shuar to understand the difficulty he was in.

At that point—and this is the moral of the story—the Shuar teammate of highest prestige within the village introduced the stranger and explained the team's mission. After that, all went well in that village. (The team visited many villages over the course of several months.)

---

# Outsiders vs. Insiders

Sometimes, charm is not enough. Arriving with the proper introductions and support is essential to developing workplace rapport.

This is especially critical if you do not fit the local people's stereotype of the foreign V.I.P. If you are not, by way of example, "the Beautiful American," but instead you are short, dark, and ugly, your initial reception may be less enthusiastic than if you fit the hosts' preconceived image. You may be a member of a minority racial or ethnic group, female, or physically disabled.

Some years ago, a bilingual school in Central America invited a specialist in teaching English as a second language to review its offerings and to suggest improvements. The teachers heard that the specialist was the director of the English Language Institute at the University of Michigan. A reception was planned to allow administrators and staff alike (an even mix of North and Central Americans) the chance to meet the specialist before he began his work. At the reception, the only stranger was a Japanese gentleman, Shigeo Imamura. "Well," began the host curriculum director, "at least you were not a kamikazi pilot." There was a nervous titter of laughter. "As a matter of fact," responded Imamura, "I was." He then told the story—in flawless English—of how he had been called to go on his solitary mission, only to be flagged down as he took his plane down the runway to take off; a more recent radar sighting had disconfirmed the target ship's location. Then, before he could be sent out on another, final, mission, the war ended, saving the lives of some 5,000 kamikaze pilots who were waiting for the solitary call to duty. They have annual reunions. Having established his credibility in English and having demonstrated in the process a fascinating personality, Imamura was off to a good start (after the first startled reception).

Some corporations play to the stereotypes. The U.S. head of one denomination of missionaries laboring in Argentina staffs the central office with tall, blond, handsome young American men. Aryans. The main duties of the central office staff were to provide logistical support to the missionaries and liaison with Argentine governmental agencies. "That's the kind of person they [the Argentines] expect to see in our missionaries and that's who I give them," said the Mission Director. The short, dark, and ugly missionaries were the ones knocking on doors and doing the core hard work of the mission.

In multicultural circles in one's native country, the stereotypes are often reversed. In the United States, for example, you expect to see African Americans or Chicanos, not Anglos, working in ethnically oriented advocacy groups. White Anglos are sometimes received with some hostility until their in-group credentials are established. This is usually

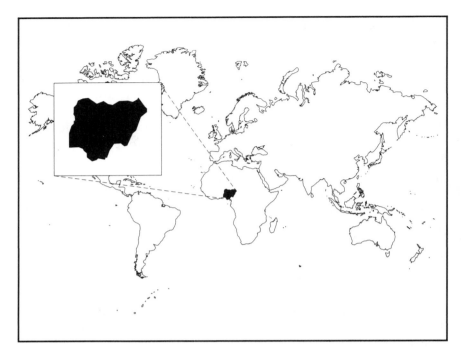

done through a critical listening to what the "outsider" has to say. It helps to have in-group attitudes and ideas.

A U.S. manager in Nigeria did not exhibit much sensitivity to in-group attitudes, as the next account painfully describes.

## A COST-EFFECTIVE REQUEST

The [nameless] U.S. manager working in Lagos needed a secretary to free him from many small, time-consuming tasks. He made his pitch for budget authorization at a meeting of upper management. Several note-taking secretaries also were in attendance.

He began his request by writing in BIG letters on the blackboard the figure of $92,600. "That," he explained, "is my yearly salary." He then broke the $92,600 down by month, by week, by day, by hour, and by minute. He wrote each figure on the board. "I need a secretary who will earn $600 a month to do many of the things I am now forced to do. At $600 per month she will be earning about six cents a minute, compared to the seventy-six cents a minute that I earn. This will result in a savings of seventy cents per minute!'' he concluded. His every minute was valuable.

His audience was speechless.

After that meeting, the U.S. manager found it difficult to have any of his ideas approved by his host peers.

# Analysis
## *What happened?*
The U.S. manager backed up his request for secretarial assistance by showing how much it would save the company.

## *What really happened?*
A year after the fact, an evaluator interviewed two Nigerian managers and one secretary who were in attendance. Their recollection of the meeting was vivid, after a fashion. Their minds had each fixated at a different point. The secretary couldn't get her eyes off the yearly salary figure occupying most of the blackboard. It blew her mind. What she or her husband could do with a salary like that! The managers followed to the point that the salary of the requested secretary was mentioned: $600 per month. That was more than they themselves earned!

## *What can Mr. Big do now?*
When there is a really big foot in your mouth, it is difficult to extract. Perhaps he could have used some good-natured humor or a disclaimer that the salary figures were not real—just illustrative. At any rate, he didn't notice that he had made a major tactical error, and no one told him. They told everybody else!

## *How can this misunderstanding be avoided in the future?*
Find out what the local salaries are before you hypothesize "an average local salary." And don't translate your worth in terms of dollars.

---

Host nationals may have an inordinate curiosity about how much you are being paid. In some cultures, you will be expected to provide this detail if you wish to be considered an in-group member. *No matter what the circumstances, do not reveal your real salary—it's just too damn high!* No matter how many expenses you list that have to be paid back home from your salary, they will not see past the astronomical salary figure.

If asked your salary by people in the host culture, instead of revealing your salary, ask them what a manager of your rank would earn in that culture. Then say that is about what you earn too, plus a little additional to cover health insurance and additional living expenses. (Be vague about how much extra for "additional" costs.) You can then go into the problem of health insurance in the United States. (If you are from Canada, the U.K., Sweden, or many other industrial countries, you may have to substitute some other cost differential.) Another approach sidesteps leaning on your high salary for professional validation as a *wunderkind* by smiling and saying your heart is full of the riches that come from a loving family.

---

## TOOLBOX
## Getting a Culturally General Fix

- Look up the GNP of the country. (*The World Bank Atlas* is a good source.)

- Ascertain the basic economy (agricultural or industrial).

- Learn how to say: "Hello"; "How are you?"; "Thank you"; "Yes"; "No."

- Become genuinely interested in the people with whom you work.

---

## TOOLBOX
## Medicating Your Own Ethnocentrism

- Don't judge the host nationals' IQs by their physical appearance or economic conditions.

- Show you assume them to be of high character and IQ by incorporating hosts into your team as advisers.

- Don't say, "Back home we do it this way."

- Eat what the host nationals eat.

┌─────────────┐
│ **TOOLBOX** │
└─────────────┘

# Establishing Credibility

- Get letters of introduction, or at least permission to use the names of mutual friends.

- Phone or send letters ahead, if time permits.

- Buy gifts for the key people (including secretaries) you will meet.

- Have selected hosts "co-author" your work. Their names on the document will help sell it to the host nationals.

There are scores of academic models to help you understand cultures in the aggregate. Each discipline develops its own constructs. One approach to gathering information about a culture that will help you modify your behavior is to identify a few critical topics that appear to be associated with different interactive styles. The next chapter will explore Hofstede's four-trait model. It can be used in situations in which you are generalizing across cultures that share a similar trait.

# 6

# Pathfinding
## *The Ins and Outs of Corporate Culture*

**Corporate culture tends to take on selected national characteristics. Knowledge of just a few of these cultural dimensions will help predict workplace behavior in many cultures. How a culture ranks on these dimensions directly affects the ease with which you will be able to establish and maintain rapport. Understanding how a particular workplace aligns on these four dimensions can help a manager or consultant find his or her way through the corporate mazeway.**

## Cultural Similarities

Many relationships can be understood, the Dutch social scientist Geert Hofstede suggests, against the backdrop of how employees in a given culture deal with four issues:

- Power distance (social inequality and relationships with authority)

- Individualism vs. collectivism (the relationship between the individual and the group)

- Assertiveness vs. modesty (concepts of aggressiveness and passivity in the interactive styles in a workplace)

- Uncertainty avoidance vs. tolerance for ambiguity

This model by Geert Hofstede was derived from empirical data—surveys of 116,000 salaried IBM employees in fifty-odd countries.

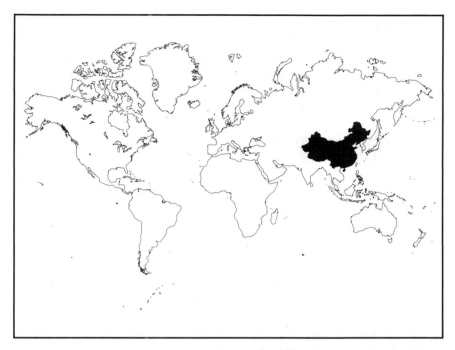

Let us see how each component of Hofstede's model may be reflected in concrete incidents.

## THE RUNAROUND: THE POWER DISTANCE INDEX

An American consultant, Eric Kong, was sent to a chemical plant in the Guangdong Province of China to determine the feasibility of a joint venture. Eric was raised in a Cantonese-speaking family in San Francisco, California, and received his engineering degree from the California Polytechnic Institute. This was his first assignment in mainland China.

The initial meetings with the plant administration were quite ceremonial. There were many flowery toasts and long, rather abstract speeches. These protocol sessions seemed to suggest an open yet uncommitted mindset. Eric scheduled several weeks after the initial flurry of ritualistic activities to talk with upper and middle management, considerably longer than he would schedule in a Western plant.

Inevitably, the managers Eric interviewed would respond in one of two ways to his requests for their opinion on details of a possible joint-venture operation. They would defer to the plant manager, or they would redirect Eric to another manager. Dutifully, Eric would approach the indicated manager, explain what he was looking for, ask his questions, and...be referred to someone else. When he approached the plant manager, he was received courteously and invited to continue to confer with the middle managers. No one seemed to be willing to offer an opinion on anything of substance.

## Analysis
### What happened?
Eric got the runaround.

### What really happened?
In companies in which there is deep consciousness of one's status, it is common for the boss to retain decision-making authority—even on issues of seemingly low priority. Often, the boss only confides in close aides, typically family members or old friends. Eric ran into a highly hierarchical company that did not delegate authority to the middle managers with whom Eric was negotiating. The way to cover your posterior when you are an employee of this type of firm is to refer decisions to others. The plant manager had the knowledge and authority to answer Eric's questions, but he wasn't ready to do that yet.

### What can Eric do now?
He can open up better lines of communication with the person or persons who make the decisions, perhaps through go-betweens. Realigning your efforts in these situations is a common occurrence, don't get discouraged.

### How can this misunderstanding be avoided in the future?
Finding the person who makes the decisions is a common plight. Sometimes finding the correct path to the decision-makers in countries that are foreign to you is a Byzantine undertaking. The results of a 1988 Gallup poll illustrate the differences between U.S. and Western European approaches to status in the workplace.

This poll surveyed opinion leaders. When asked to respond to the question of whether the society "places a great importance on social position," only 13 percent of U.S. opinion leaders agreed, versus 70 percent of the Western Europeans. The difference in response to the statement, "gives everyone an equal opportunity to succeed," was even more dramatic: 81 percent of the Americans agreed, while only 4 percent of the Western Europeans agreed. Few businesspersons anticipate the extent of the differences in corporate culture within industrial nations. In the case of China, centuries of hierarchical rule under emperors imbues the workplace more strongly than the egalitarianism professed by socialist rule.

### *What are some of the characteristics of countries that tend to score high (and low) on the power distance index?*

- Small (vs. large) middle class

- Privileges for the powerful (vs. equal rights for all)

- Powerful people try to look as impressive as possible (vs. powerful people try to look less powerful)

- Autocracy or oligarchy (vs. majority-vote government)

- High (vs. low) level of stratification by status

### *How do countries tend to score on the power distance index?*

According to Hofstede, a typical workplace in Australia, Austria, Canada, Costa Rica, Denmark, Germany, Great Britain, Israel, Netherlands, New Zealand, Republic of Ireland, Scandinavia, Switzerland, and the United States tend to score on the low side of the power distance index.

Scoring high on the power distance index are Ecuador, Egypt, Ghana, Guatemala, India, Indonesia, Iraq, Kuwait, Lebanon, Libya, Malaysia, Mexico, Nigeria, Panama, the Philippines, Saudia Arabia, Sierra Leone, United Arab Emirates, and Venezuela.

### *Rating an organization for placement on the power distance index*

If a workplace scores "yes" on three of the four questions in the Toolbox on page 82, the workplace scores high on the power differentiation index. If the workplace scores "no" on three of the four, the workplace is high

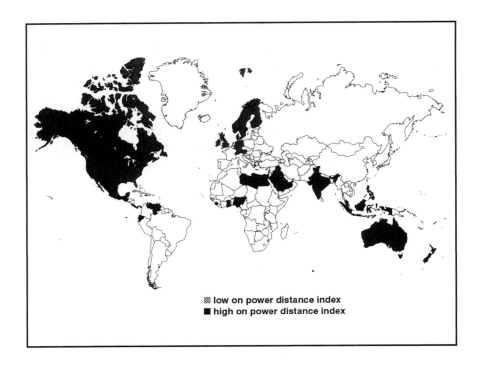

- low on power distance index
- high on power distance index

on the egalitarian side of the index (that is, low on power difference). (The scales used in this chapter have been altered and abbreviated from Hofstede's scales; consequently, they do not have research equivalence.)

---

**TOOLBOX**

## Identifying High Power-Distance Organizations

- Are employees often afraid to express disagreement with their managers?

- Do subordinates believe their boss's decision-making style is autocratic and/or paternalistic?

- Do subordinates prefer for their boss to make the decisions, or do they (subordinates) prefer to have a consultative role?

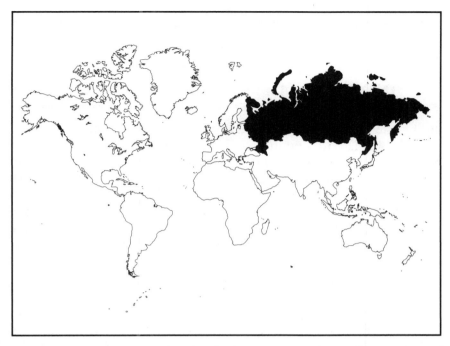

- Do the highest paid individuals earn more than 20 times that of the lowest paid?

### *What initial relationship-building strategies can you develop when you find yourself in a workplace that scores high (or low) on the power distance index?*

The first issue is how do *you* place on this continuum? If you find that your own communicative preferences differ substantially from those of your corporate setting, you will have to stretch a bit, especially if you are out of practice working in this type of setting.

If your international workplace scores high on the power index, this suggests that working through the chain of command is very important in that setting.

---

The second corporate culture trait Hofstede identifies concerns how individual- vs. collective-minded the culture is. Sometimes the process of getting to know the other person requires reaching out on a personal level. The next account illustrates this.

# CULTIVATING RUSSIAN RELATIONSHIPS: THE INDIVIDUALISM-COLLECTIVISM INDEX

In the aftermath of *perestroika*, a British engineering firm struck a deal with the Russians to support them in a plant start-up. This plant would produce active wear (sweatshirts and pants) for the domestic Russian market. To staff this demanding project, the firm had contracted two Britons, Diana and Horace. These two English speakers would use interpreters. There was an unfilled slot for another engineer. Nigel Johnson had the luck of being the only one in the firm to speak the language of the Motherland. His involvement came at a time when the infrastructure had been set up and all that remained was the challenging productivity development stage of the project. The young Brit left Manchester for the two-day journey.

In Russia, the expectation is that consultants are tall, light-skinned, white-haired individuals with considerable wrinkles; wisdom tempered by experience and age. In an evening meeting with a middle-aged British colleague before his first day at the plant in Russia, Nigel (who is short, dark, and young) was told, diplomatically, of course, that there may be a problem. "Don't worry about that," Nigel replied. "I'll take care of it." He had been debriefed before his departure on the tense relations between the Russian director, the American joint-venture partner (responsible for supplying materials and equipment), and the British engineering firm which was providing technical support in the start-up. Two things that he had going for him were his knowledge of the Russian language and Russian culture.

The next day, Nigel began establishing a relationship with the plant manager and the supervisors. Speaking to them in Russian, he introduced himself, talked about his family, answered questions, and asked them about themselves. Had Nigel fit the V.I.P. stereotype, he would have begun his consultancy with some credibility, but since he did not, he established a relationship that allowed the host professionals to give him the chance to establish his competence.

Nigel's own supervisor, an Englishman, tried to get Nigel back on track.

"Nigel, it seems you can be making better use of your time. Can you give me a weekly schedule of how you plan to divide your time between the instructors and supervisors? This way we won't get in each other's way."

# Analysis
## *What happened?*
The supervisor observed Nigel talking about personal things to the Russian workers and thought that this was a waste of time. The supervisor's attitude was, "We are paying him a hell of a lot of money, why is he wasting time?" To get things back on track (according to his lights), the supervisor tried to structure Nigel's time: "What will you be doing between 8:00 A.M. and 9:00 A.M.?"

## *What really happened?*
Nigel's supervisor had internalized the business etiquette of many industrialized nations. Namely, it is considered a courtesy not to waste the other person's time. As Benjamin Franklin admonished, "Time is money." The teaching of business in many U.S. universities, for instance, reflects this philosophy by teaching a method of business communication called the direct plan approach. In this approach, you focus the discussion by beginning your message with the most important information placed up front. The objective is to go straight to the point. This approach is perceived to have an additional advantage because it prevents your message from getting lost in the "clutter" of later messages. In the case of written communication, information at the end of a business message may never even be read.

Nigel recognized that Russians are very relationship oriented, so he spent considerable time during his first days on-site with the management, first-line supervisors, and instructors talking about his family, his perceptions of Russia, and his previous projects while delicately answering questions, such as "Life in England is much easier than here, isn't it?" Nigel went out of his way to avoid putting down the host country. He also talked to many people he would not work with until later in the project. This process allowed the Russians to begin to feel comfortable with him as a person. Nigel would need their trust later to learn what they felt were some of their biggest problems.

## What can Nigel do now?

Nigel revealed his strategy to his supervisor. In this case, the supervisor had faith in Nigel and deferred to his preferred working style. (It does not always work out this way.)

A few days after Nigel's arrival, he was called into a meeting of management and supervisors where his advice was asked on a particular problem. Although the plant director did not agree with Nigel's advice, he did say how glad he was that Nigel was there to help. Nigel had received the plant director's blessing. Reaching out on a personal level had paid off.

## How can this clash of styles be avoided in the future?

Russia tends to be more relationship oriented than is the custom in the United Kingdom or the United States. The attitude in many industrial nations is to get down to business and not waste the other person's time. This task-oriented mentality (''business first, then pleasure'') can impede establishing rapport with relationship-oriented cultures that hold the view that ''pleasure'' (i.e., probing another person's character through socialization) should come first. Relationship-oriented cultures often lengthen the business communication with the objective of getting to know and trust those with whom you will work. Russian emphasis on relationships is shared by many countries, especially developing nations.

Nigel anticipated the need to put socialization before business because he had worked in Russia previously and because he had learned that in certain countries time spent developing relationships paid off. But how does someone not familiar with the culture anticipate which work style will be more productive, task orientation or relationship orientation?

The easiest basis on which to guess the preferred interactive style is to hypothesize that the higher the average GNP per capita, the more task-oriented the interactive style tends to be; the lower the average GNP per capita, the more relationship-oriented the preferred style tends to be. (At the time of Nigel's visit, Russia had a per capita GNP of about $2,700, which places Russia in the middle ranges.)

The World Bank annually reports on the GNP per capita for 207 countries. The map on page 87 shows that the twenty-one countries with the highest GNP per capita (over $15,000 [US$ 1992]) are, in alphabetical order: Australia, Belgium, Canada, Denmark, Finland, France, Germany, Hong Kong, Iceland, Italy, Japan, Luxembourg, Netherlands, Norway, Qatar (oil, not industry), Singapore, Sweden, Switzerland,

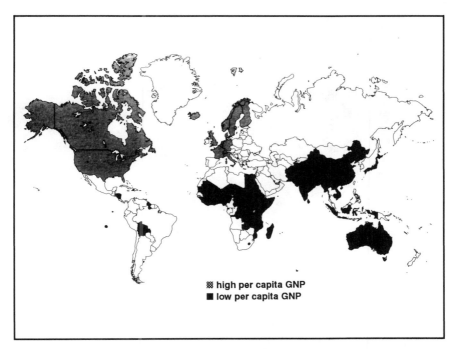

high per capita GNP
low per capita GNP

United Arab Emirates (oil, not industry), United Kingdom, and the United States. The two economies mostly dependent on oil can be expected to have anomalous traits. You can hypothesize that the other nineteen countries will prefer a task-oriented approach.

The map shows that the fifty-seven countries with the lowest average GNP per capita (less than $700 [US$ 1992], including nine that are based on World Bank estimates) are, in alphabetical order: Afghanistan, Bangladesh, Benin, Bhutan, Bolivia, Bosnia and Herzegovina, Burkina Faso, Burundi, Cambodia, Central African Republic, Chad, China, Comoros, Côte d'Ivoire, Egypt, Equatorial Guinea, Eritrea, Ethiopia, Gambia, Ghana, Guinea, Guinea-Bissau, Guyana, Haiti, Honduras, India, Indonesia, Kenya, Lao PDR, Lesotho, Liberia, Madagascar, Malawi, Maldives, Mali, Mauritania, Mozambique, Myanmar, Nepal, Nicaragua, Niger, Nigeria, Pakistan, Rwanda, São Tomé and Principe, Sierra Leone, Somalia, Sri Lanka, Sudan, Tajikistan, Tanzania, Togo, Uganda, Viet Nam, Zaire, Zambia, Zimbabwe. You can hypothesize that these fifty-seven countries will prefer a relationship-oriented approach.

The remaining 128 countries fall somewhere between an average per capita GNP of $700 and $15,000. This represents quite a range; countries

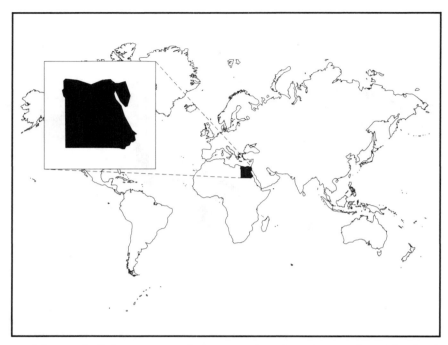

at either end of the range can be expected to share interactive styles (task oriented vs. relationship oriented) with other countries nearest to them in terms of average per capita GNP. There will, of course, be exceptions.

Another factor to consider is that the international manager or consultant is an outsider, an unknown entity. It is not hard to justify taking a little time to get to know the people you will be working with and to give them a chance to size you up.

---

The next account illustrates another disquieting symptom on the individualism-collectivism index.

# TEA AND BISCUITS: THE INDIVIDUALISM-COLLECTIVISM INDEX

Having just arrived in Egypt two days earlier, Cal was still experiencing more than a spot of jet lag as he taxied through dense traffic to the train station. All the seats on the early morning express from Cairo to the Mediterranean city named after Alexander the Great had been sold, so Cal had to wait for the next train, a local. It experienced motor problems and pulled into Alexandria almost an hour behind its scheduled arrival. After checking into a hotel and dropping off his luggage, Cal took a cab to the university where he was to spend several days evaluating a fifteen-year-old center that designed and staffed a program to teach special English classes for students of, respectively, sciences, business, and medicine. Although his visit was expected, he arrived three hours late.

Upon arrival, the deputy head of the center, an Egyptian woman, welcomed him and introduced him to several Egyptian and British members of the teaching staff. Although the deputy would be available for the rest of the day, her Egyptian colleagues by then could only spare another hour. They repaired to a conference room, and tea/coffee/soda orders were taken. The program had never been evaluated, and the staff was nervous. Cal began by asking the staff to describe the program.

Because of a shortage of textbooks written in Arabic for many of the courses taught in the university, English textbooks were used. Although the students had studied English as a second language in secondary school, they naturally had difficulty deciphering the college textbooks written in English. The courses Cal was evaluating were designed to teach the kind of English as a second language (ESL) that would make it easier for students to understand the textbooks.

Cal interrupted the description frequently to ask clarifying questions. The tea arrived in a small vessel without a handle. While waiting for the tea to cool a bit, Cal asked to see the objectives for each course. They were not at hand but would be made available the next morning. He then asked if he could see the textual materials that had been prepared for the special English courses.

"How do the English materials in your courses complement the English textbooks that the professors use?" Cal asked. He was informed that the English selections used in the materials had been taken directly from the English textbooks. Since the English textbooks had been prepared for native speakers of English who were university students (they were not designed to become bestsellers on the mass market), Cal asked questions about the reading level of the materials. They were difficult for him to read. Cal probed the content validity of the special English supplements. "Do the reading selections bring into focus points that are central to an understanding of the subject matter?" He was told that the ESL teachers were not geology teachers; they were English teachers. "Has the staff consulted with geology professors to identify the main concepts of the regular course taught in Arabic so that the English selections that are used in the English course will provide help with understanding of the key concepts rather than of peripheral material?" They replied that in the Egyptian university system it was difficult to talk to the professors.

Cal asked to see the tests that were used to measure student achievement. It became quickly apparent that no item analysis had been performed and that their reliability had not been established. Cal tried to make the staff aware of the importance of doing this. The staff defended the usefulness of the tests in their present form.

At the end of the session, one of the Egyptian staff members voiced her frustration.

"This is not how to go about an evaluation," she began. "You have been disrespectful and have jumped all around. You have not read the background materials. You have not introduced yourself properly. We would have liked to drink tea together and get to know you better."

## Analysis
### What happened?
The consultant had not properly introduced himself.

### What really happened?
In attempting to make up for lost time, Cal combined tea-drinking formalities with pointed work-oriented questions. He omitted, unfortunately, the kinds of personal exchanges that normally accompany the tea-drinking phase of discussions. The hosts had not been given the chance to develop a sense of the intentions of the consultant, and they became unduly defensive.

### What can Cal do now?
One way to undo some of the damage would have been to extend his schedule by staying on at this site for longer than planned, taking time to cultivate the desirable personal relationships. Cal did not feel he had time to do this, however. Cal did try to mitigate the frustration felt by the hosts by spending an hour or so at the close of his evaluation with the project director, giving him a more complete debriefing, and going

out of his way to try to smooth relations by apologizing for his error of protocol and expressing personal appreciation for the dedication to the project of the host team and for their frankness in expressing their frustration. Overall, Cal found the project to be doing especially well. This improved the situation, but it did not dissolve all of the hard feelings.

### How can this misunderstanding be avoided in the future?

Triandis, Brislin, and Hui provide succinct advice for people crossing the individual-collective divide.

> . . . [C]ollectivists who interact extensively with individualists find that they have to learn to talk about personal accomplishments; to establish short-term relationships (a network); to pay more attention to contracts; to engage in fewer superordinate and subordinate behaviors depending on others' status levels; and to communicate why certain collective behaviors must take place to maintain a sense of self worth.
>
> Individualists who interact extensively with collectivists find that they have to pay attention to people's group memberships to understand behaviors which take place; to develop long-term relationships based on trust; to criticize very carefully, only when necessary and never when a person may lose face in front of members of the collective; to understand illicit behavior which benefits the collective but puts out-groups at a disadvantage; and to be more sensitive to status hierarchies.

### What are some of the characteristics of countries that tend to score high on the individualism side of the individualism-collectivism index?

- Honest people speak their minds (vs. good people maintain harmony and avoid direct confrontations).

- Hiring and promotion are based on merit (vs. charity starts at home; give your family and friends a break).

- Management is management of individuals (vs. management of groups).

- Task is more important than relationships (vs. relationships prevail over tasks).

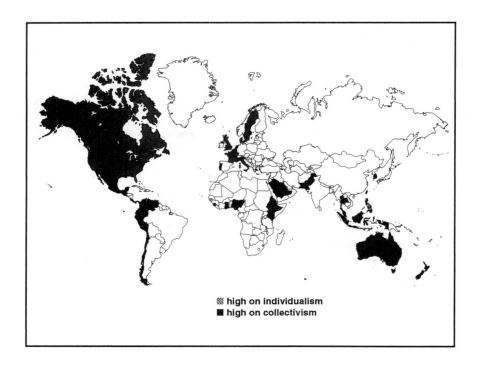

&#x2737; high on individualism
&#x25A0; high on collectivism

- Everyone thinks self-actualization is the ultimate goal (vs. everyone seeks harmony and consensus in society as ultimate goals).

- High (vs. low) per capita GNP.

- High level of freedom of the press (vs. the press controlled by the state).

### How do countries tend to score on the individualism-collectivism index?

Countries that tend to score high on the collective end of the continuum include Chile, Colombia, Costa Rica, Ecuador, El Salvador, Ethiopia, Ghana, Guatemala, Indonesia, Kenya, Malaysia, Mexico, Nigeria, Pakistan, Panama, Peru, the Philippines, Portugal, Sierra Leone, Singapore, South Korea, Taiwan, Tanzania, Thailand, Venezuela, and Zambia.

Scoring high on the individual end of the continuum are Australia, Belgium, Canada, Denmark, France, Great Britain, Italy, Netherlands, New Zealand, Sweden, and the United States,

*Rating an organization for placement on the*
*individualism-collectivism index*

If both of the statements listed in the Toolbox below seem to characterize the target workplace, that workplace scores high on the individualism index. If neither statement appears to describe the workplace, the workplace scores high on the collectivism side of the index (that is, low on individualism).

---

### TOOLBOX

## Identifying Highly Individualized Organizations

1. The country is wealthy.

2. If they had to choose, most employees would feel that it is more important to have a job that . . .

   a. gives you a lot of freedom to adopt your own approach to the job and

      gives you challenging work to do,

   **rather than** to have a job that . . .

   b. provides training opportunities to improve your skills or to learn new skills and

      has good physical working conditions.

---

*What initial relationship-building strategies can you*
*develop when you find yourself in a workplace that*
*scores high (or low) on the individualism-*
*collectivism index?*

First, will the way *you* place on this continuum require you to make a special effort to work within a workplace setting with different characteristics?

In work settings that are high on the individualism continuum, go about your work from a task-oriented perspective. In highly collective

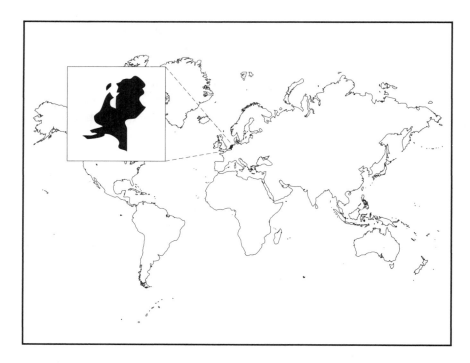

settings, go out of your way to acknowledge the importance of the interaction of the particular individuals and group that inhabit the workplace.

The next account relates to the third cultural trait identified by Hofstede, the assertive-modesty continuum. It is important in developing relationships.

# ESTABLISHING YOUR QUALIFICATIONS: THE ASSERTIVENESS-MODESTY INDEX

Geert Hofstede relates an event that happened to him when he was a young man in the Netherlands interviewing for a junior manager position with an American engineering firm located there. He had sent the firm a brief letter stating his interest and qualifications for the job, and had enclosed a one-page résumé identifying his excellent academic background and previous engineering work at a prestigious Dutch company.

At the interview, Geert was, as the Dutch are taught to be, polite and modest. He waited for the American interviewer to ask questions that would probe his qualifications. But the interviewer did not ask the expected questions. Instead, the American asked some detailed questions about tool design—questions that required a knowledge of specialized words in English—and other issues that are generally learned on the job during the first few weeks of employment. Geert considered them irrelevant. At the end of an interview that Geert, many years later, still recalls as "painful," the American told him that they needed "a first-class man" for the position.

## Analysis
### *What happened?*
The interview went poorly and Geert was found lacking in qualifications for the job.

### *What really happened?*
Geert acted modestly—an engaging virtue in countries that value this trait—anticipating the opportunity to reveal his qualifications at the interview by answering well-phrased questions put to him by the interviewer. Instead, the American interviewer was looking for the candidate to sell himself more aggressively as a "can-do" prospect. The American equated a modest approach with inexperience and lack of leadership potential.

### *What could Geert do now?*
Nothing. He (and the interviewer) blew the interview. More often than not in this type of situation, we never do figure out what went wrong.

### *How can this misunderstanding be avoided in the future?*
Geert Hofstede himself answers the question in his pathfinding research. When workplace interactions occur within a culture that values modesty over assertiveness, you should understate your personal qualifications and expect questions from those with whom you are interacting that will

enable you to elaborate on relevant areas. For workplaces that value assertiveness over modesty, you should make an effort to sell yourself as well qualified for the task at hand.

For managers and consultants who find themselves in an ambiguous situation where it is not clear which approach is valued more highly, perhaps it may be advisable to begin with a low-keyed approach (that is, modest), then, if it appears the interviewer is not asking the kind of questions that enable you to elaborate on your ability to do the job, take more initiative in providing relevant information. It is a good idea to carry two résumés: one brief; the other, a more detailed résumé to be held in reserve. If you know someone with experience in dealing with the target firm, he or she may be able to head you in the right direction.

Once you are working in the target organization, find a well-informed colleague to orient you. The Toolbox on page 97 can help you ask the right questions.

### *What are some of the characteristics of countries that tend to score high on the assertiveness side of the assertiveness-modesty index?*

- Material success and progress are strong societal values (vs. caring for others).

- Men are supposed to be ambitious and tough (vs. everybody is supposed to be modest).

- One lives to work (vs. works to live).

- Managers are expected to be decisive (vs. skilled in striving for consensus).

- Few (vs. many) women are in elected political positions.

### *Which countries tend to score high on the assertiveness-modesty index?*

Countries that Hofstede identifies as high on the assertiveness end of the continuum are Austria, Germany, Great Britain, Italy, Jamaica, Japan, Mexico, Republic of Ireland, South Africa, Switzerland, United States, and Venezuela.

Countries that tend to score high on the modesty side of the continuum are Chile, Costa Rica, Denmark, Finland, Guatemala, Netherlands, Norway, Portugal, South Korea, Sweden, Thailand, and Uruguay.

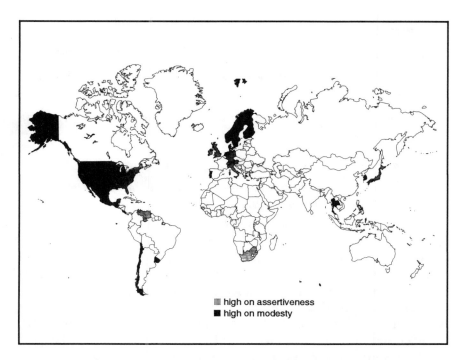

 high on assertiveness
■ high on modesty

### *Rating an organization for placement on the assertiveness-modesty index*

If the workplace is better characterized by *a* (in the Toolbox below), then the workplace scores high on assertiveness index. If it is better characterized by *b*, then the workplace scores high on the modesty side of the index.

---

**TOOLBOX**

# Identifying Highly Assertive Organizations

If they had to choose, most employees would prefer a job that . . .

a. has an opportunity for high earnings,

gives you the recognition you deserve when you do a good job, and that

gives you a chance for advancement to higher level jobs,

**rather than** a job in which . . .

b. you have a good working relationship with your direct superior,

you work with people who cooperate well with each other, and where

you have job security; you can work with the company for as long as you want.

*What initial relationship-building strategies can you develop when you find yourself in a workplace that scores high on the modesty side of the assertiveness-modesty index?*

Again, how do *you* place on this continuum?

U.S. managers and consultants (along with those from the other eleven countries listed on page 96) more often than not have spent most of their time in organizations that score high in assertiveness. In dealing with organizations that score low on the assertiveness dimension (that is, organizations that score high on the modesty side of the continuum), outsider managers and consultants will want to avoid seeming crass and overly materialistic. In searching for ways to motivate staff, they will want to look at team building and security issues rather than to emphasize competitiveness and merit bonuses.

---

The fourth trait of corporate culture that Hofstede identifies as key to predicting interactive styles, uncertainty avoidance, is embedded in the next account.

# FROM BLACK BREAD TO TORTILLAS: THE UNCERTAINTY AVOIDANCE-TOLERANCE FOR AMBIGUITY INDEX

One engineer, Curt, working on a plant start-up for a Russian firm in the chilly wastelands of Siberia experienced a jarring, geopolitical contrast when he finished the start-up only to begin another plant start-up in the northern part of sunny Mexico.

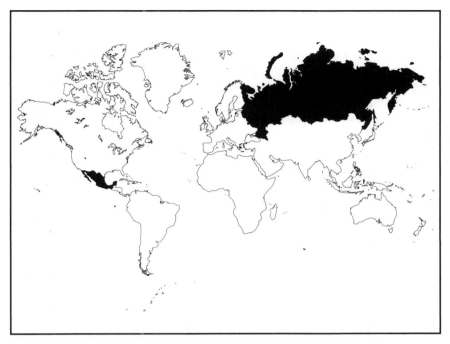

It had taken several weeks to adjust to working with the Russian people (his previous assignment had been in rural, southern United States). Russian culture tended to be high context, although the plant also had low-context characteristics—ideas, not individuals, were criticized, for example. Curt found that he worked most effectively by painting a picture for Russian management of what the work system would look like after implementing his suggested programs. For example, part of the infrastructure would include a trained support staff in the form of instructors and supervisors to support the operators on the shop floor.

Curt began his efforts by training the instructors in proven procedures to train new operators in the appropriate work methods to achieve high levels of production with good quality. These sessions would not have any fixed time schedule. Curt would call the group together at various times of the day to discuss common problems that the instructors were having. He did the same with the supervisors who worked with some of the more experienced operators.

The Russian plant director was comfortable with this sort of training with no set time schedule. In regular weekly meetings with his department heads, he received most of the feedback he was looking for. The department heads were pleased with Curt's help. Curt continued to solidify the infrastructure with this approach and left the Siberian *taiga* with a satisfied client.

In Curt's next assignment to the northern semidesert region of Mexico, however, the appropriate approach was completely different. In the first few days on-site, Curt quickly became aware of the need for management and the support staff to have a detailed schedule of the training activities. They were not comfortable without a great level of detail. Nonetheless, as is common in plant start-ups, the schedule for the planned activities often has to change because delays in raw materials and equipment affect the activities you are able to carry out.

# Analysis
## *What happened?*
In order to get the desired results and client satisfaction in both Russia and Mexico, Curt had to change his approach and adjust his training techniques to accommodate different cultural preferences. One was comfortable with a loose schedule, the other wanted detailed schedules.

## *What really happened?*
Curt went from working in a factory with an experienced workforce where there was a high tolerance for ambiguity (Russia) to a workplace with an inexperienced workforce where there was a low tolerance for ambiguity (Mexico).

## *What can Curt do now?*
Curt did what he needed to do. He recognized the need in the Mexican plant for planning schedules, and he provided them. If he had chosen to work in the same manner as he had in the Russian plant with a much less "structured" approach, the Mexican client would not have felt the same confidence in the work that was being done.

## *How can this misunderstanding be avoided in the future?*
Recognize that methods that work in one country do not necessarily work in another. As this example illustrates, an outsider coming into another working environment needs to be aware of this and to look for methods that do work. Do not be bull-headed and restrict yourself to doing things in a way "you know will work."

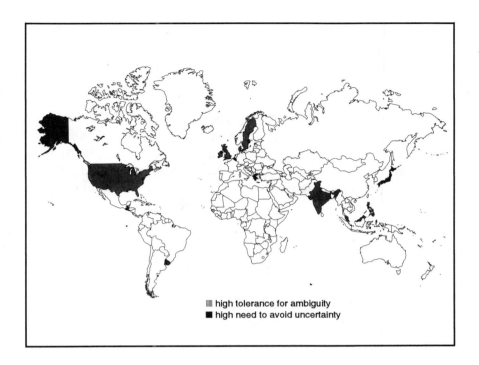

| | |
|---|---|
| ▥ | high tolerance for ambiguity |
| ■ | high need to avoid uncertainty |

### *What are some of the characteristics of countries that tend to score high (and low) on the uncertainty avoidance index?*

- Citizens are negative (vs. positive) toward institutions.

- Attitudes are negative (vs. positive) toward young people.

- Nationalism, xenophobia, and repression of minorities (vs. regionalism, internationalism, and integration of minorities) is common.

- Reliance on experts and specialists (vs. reliance on generalists and common sense).

### *Which countries tend to score high (and low) on the uncertainty avoidance index?*

Countries that tend to score high in uncertainty avoidance, according to Hofstede, are Belgium, El Salvador, Greece, Guatemala, Japan, Portugal, and Uruguay.

Countries that score low in their need to avoid uncertainty (that is, they score high in their tolerance for ambiguity) include Denmark, Great Britain, India, Jamaica, Malaysia, the Philippines, Republic of Ireland, Singapore, Sweden, and the United States.

### *Rating an organization for placement on the uncertainty avoidance-tolerance of ambiguity index*

If employees tend to agree with all three statements in the Toolbox below, the workplace scores high on the uncertainty index. If they do not agree with any of the three, the workplace scores high on the other side of the continuum, tolerance of ambiguity.

---

| TOOLBOX |

## Identifying Organizations with a High Need to Avoid Uncertainty

Most employees would agree that . . .

> company rules should not be broken, even when an employee thinks it is in the company's best interest,
>
> you plan to stay with the company for more than five years, perhaps until you retire,
>
> you often feel nervous or tense at work.

### *What initial relationship-building strategies can you develop when you find yourself in a workplace that scores high (or low) on the uncertainty avoidance index?*

Does *your* placement on this continuum raise any special issues for you when you work in a setting with a very different style?

If you come from a background characterized by a high tolerance of ambiguity and find yourself in a workplace that scores high in needing to avoid uncertainty, you will want to be more explicit than usual in your instructions. If you want people in the workforce (perhaps supervisors) to be more creative in their response to new situations, then go out of your way to reassure them you value their judgment and introduce brainstorming (and other) techniques that place a premium on creativity. If you encourage them to take risks, then reward the risk-taking regardless of whether it works out. In other words, do not come down hard on them when they make inevitable mistakes.

While additional predictive power is possible by determining the precise combination of the four cultural traits in your workplace, the fifteen possible combinations—using only high or low ratings—makes this somewhat impractical. The toolboxes presented in this chapter provide an awareness that will make crossing cultural boundaries easier.

---

## Navigating Uncharted Waters

What are some of the main points to be inferred from this chapter? Since managers and consultants often arrive at their assignments without much of a sense of the local plant or agency, sitting down with several people shortly after arrival and eliciting their sense of things can help the work proceed more efficiently.

One should note that multinational companies also tend to reflect some of the culture of the parent firm. This is especially evident in countries where women are not granted equal opportunities in the workplace. In Japan and Mexico, to take two such examples, women managers are not uncommon in U.S.-owned firms.

This cultural-trait approach is helpful for predicting behavior that will enhance rapport with host nationals, but there are many critical behaviors you need to master in your cultural comings and goings, and no theoretical construct will provide enough of the answers. You need to learn the specific ritual behaviors yourself. You can be sure that there are do's and don'ts for each culture in which you interact. The next chapter illustrates these.

# 7

# That Magic Something Called Rapport
## *Using the Proper Protocols*

The same event in two cultures often has very different significance. Differing habits governing eye contact can provoke disastrous cross-cultural misunderstandings. Christmas may occasion a one- or two-day holiday in a U.S. factory, and a ten- to fifteen-day holiday in a factory in Mexico. Hello and goodbye protocols can depend on cues that are difficult for an outsider to discern. Tasks that are totally appropriate for anyone in one country are seen as demeaning for certain strata (white collar workers, for example) in another culture. Seemingly trivial cultural differences (for example, where to put the towel after you bathe) can carry severe repercussions. Differing rules of table etiquette or improper practices of social deference can be a real turn-off.

## Magic Rituals

There is a magic word that children are taught by their mothers in the English-speaking world. It makes things happen. And if you don't say it, you get into trouble with your mother. The word, of course, is *please*. Each society has its own magic words and its own magic rites. If you don't follow them, you get into trouble. The epithet "arrogant" may be hurled—implicitly or explicitly—at boundary crossers who neglect to follow the conventions.

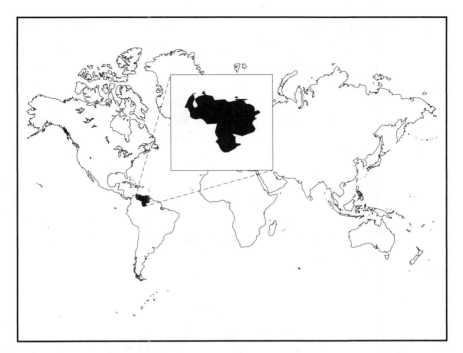

Each society has ritual behaviors that oil the social and business machinery. These often consist of discrete behaviors (for instance, eating with only your right hand) that are required for acceptance into a culture, including both entry into a new culture and reentry into one's first culture after a long sojourn abroad. How do we get a sense of which ritualistic behaviors are critical for gaining acceptance, and—the other side of the coin—which behaviors provoke undesired stress among members of the host culture?

As international voyagers, we need strategies that reduce the friction the *host nationals* experience as we interact with them under what may be for us new ground rules. We also need to look out for frictions our own *compatriots* may experience when we return home sporting exotic behaviors.

How do we learn which ritualistic behaviors aid in gaining acceptance in a culture and which ones provoke undesired stress among members of the host culture? Let us profit from the sweat of others. (Reading this book is a good start.)

# MISFOCUSED RESPECT

Sara, the cashier of the local branch of a U.S.-owned detergent manufacturing company needed to see the plant manager about her vacation schedule. The U.S. manager, Mr. Hillup, sat behind the desk in his office while Sara explained her wishes. When Sara left the meeting, she was seething.

A coworker asked her if Mr. Hillup had denied her request for her preferred vacation dates.

"Oh, he approved that, all right, but he treated me disrespectfully."

"What did he do?"

"First, he didn't say *buenas tardes* or *qué se le ofrece* (what can I do for you?), he just waited for me to begin talking. Then while I was talking, he didn't look me in the eye; he just looked around the room. He seemed to be making a point of showing he was not interested in my concerns."

## Analysis
### *What happened?*
From Sara's perspective, the manager showed disinterest and disrespect in the way he had received her.

### *What really happened?*
The important rituals of courteous interaction in Latin America differ from those of the United States. Mr. Hillup, having arrived at his position of plant manager directly from a similar position in the United States, had not learned the appropriate etiquette for meetings with his Venezuelan staff. In fact, he was not aware that there were any differences.

### *What can Mr. Hillup do now?*
Mr. Hillup did not realize that Sara was furious, and remained angry for some days. As was appropriate while interacting with her boss, Sara had swallowed her personal feelings while she was in his presence (but exploded when she was in the company of her peers). Nobody wants to give the boss bad news, much less news of personal inadequacy, so Mr. Hillup remained ignorant of the problem. Fortunately, he was a particularly effective bottom-line manager and was respected for this by his employees. Consequently, in spite of suffering many personal humilia-

tions, his staff remained efficient. One wonders how much better they would have been had the interpersonal quality of the workplace improved from the top.

### How can this misunderstanding be avoided in the future?

Foreign managers and consultants cannot rely solely on observation to learn the requisite workplace etiquette. This is so for two reasons. First, we observe selectively. We don't see cues that our cultural upbringing renders subtle or irrelevant. Second, since Mr. Hillup entered the workplace as a high-status person (plant manager) and as a foreigner, he was "protected" from much of the social reality that governs the behavior of local people. Consequently, foreign managers must make a special effort to ask questions, perhaps of a host national mentor, to discern critical patterns of effective interaction.

There are some general guidelines that help produce effective interpersonal communications within and outside the workplace. A productive approach to building and sustaining relationships is to try to be "confirming" in our interactions. Evelyn Sieburg has studied what she calls "disconfirming" and "confirming" communication. Confirming behaviors are those that cause the other person to value himself or herself as an individual, and disconfirming behaviors cause the other person to question his or her self-worth.

---

# Sieburg's Disconfirming and Confirming Responses

Disconfirming Responses (stated egocentrically):

- *Impervious response*: Fails to recognize the remarks we just made.

- *Interrupting response*: The other person begins to talk before we have finished what we are saying.

- *Irrelevant response*: One that seems to have nothing to do with the ideas or feelings we have just expressed.

- *Tangential response*: When someone responds to our remarks by acknowledging what we just said and then quickly shifts to a new and quite different topic. This tends to be less disconfirming because it does, minimally, recognize our communication.

- *Impersonal response*: One that makes us feel as if we were part of a large audience, instead of in an interpersonal setting. The individual we are talking with responds to us with a speech that seems designed not for us, but for anyone who will listen.

- *Incongruous response*: When what is said is at odds with how it is said. For example, "I had a good time at your party" said without any conviction is an incongruous response.

Confirming Responses:

- *Direct acknowledgment*: Recognizing the other person's remarks and reacting directly to them by saying something that represents a direct response to those remarks.

- *Agreement about content*: Agreeing with the ideas, attitudes, opinions, or beliefs expressed by another person. Disagreement may not be confirming, but since it clearly acknowledges the other person's communication, it is not disconfirming either.

- *Supportive response*: Supporting another person by responding to his or her statements with understanding or reassurance.

- *Clarifying response*: Either focuses on the content or on the feelings that are expressed. We clarify by elaborating on what the other person has said, by asking for more information, and by saying something that enables the other person to expand on his or her remarks.

- *Expression of positive feeling*: "I like your ideas" or "I'm excited about your plans" are examples.

Even on your own turf, sensitivity and knowledge of other cultures can prevent profound resentment.

# A DEATH IN THE FAMILY

In a factory in a western suburb of Chicago, one of the workers, Ramón, asked his boss for permission to attend a funeral the next day. The supervisor, Tom Dolittle, asked who had died.

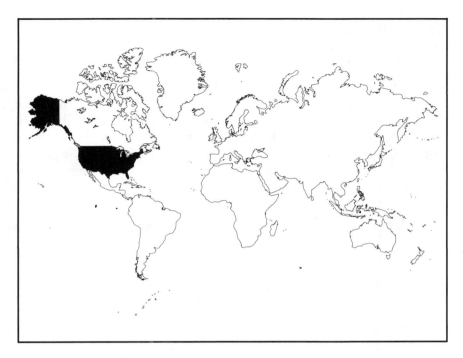

"My *compadre*," replied Ramón.

"What was his relation to you?"

"He was my *compadre*."

"What's a *compadre*?" asked Tom.

"It's like a very special friend," explained Ramón.

"Sorry. We only allow absences to attend the funerals of the immediate family—parents and children. Company policy."

"But everyone expects me to be there. We're *compadres*."

"Sorry. Company policy."

## Analysis
### *What happened?*

A worker tried to take time from work for the funeral of a friend, but it was against company policy.

### *What really happened?*

Kinship ties in the Hispanic world extend beyond the nuclear family. A sense of "family" includes grandparents, aunts and uncles, cousins, godfathers, and the especially close relationship known as the *compadre*.

Not attending the funeral for one of these people in your extended family would cause acute family distress.

## *What can Tom do now?*

He should, while there is still time to reverse his refusal, ask someone who understands Hispanic culture whether he did the right thing. If company policy is inflexible, he should move to make it more sensitive to employees from diverse cultures. Funerals are important to many people beyond the nuclear family, and in many cultures you will hurt feelings (not the least of which are your own) by not attending the service.

## *How can this misunderstanding be avoided in the future?*

Unless you are managing a union-free sweatshop with potential employees lined up around the block, many policies—including compassionate leave—need to be reexamined by multiethnic representatives of the workforce, with the objective of making recommendations that do not provoke cross-cultural resentment.

---

How was Tom supposed to know this? Many, if not most, discrete behaviors that are prerequisites for acceptance into a society are not predictable from larger cultural themes. Some of these are so idiosyncratic that you have to learn them from people (or publications) that describe "quaint" customs of a certain society. Some examples of this are the topics of conversation to avoid (in Thailand, politics, religion, and the royal family); good table manners (in China, never refuse the bear's paw soup); and while living in a host home, when to keep your bedroom door open (in Latin America you generally keep it open all during the day and much of the evening, as well—and the room neat and you properly dressed). Personal experience as a sojourner in the culture will reveal some of these critical behaviors, but not by any means all of them.

There are thousands of other examples of this level of behavior, behavior that is not adequately foreshadowed by any extant model. They include (and are described below) the cue for ending a social visit in India and in an upper-Amazon tribe, and the proper etiquette in parts of Colombia for placing your towel after you have bathed.

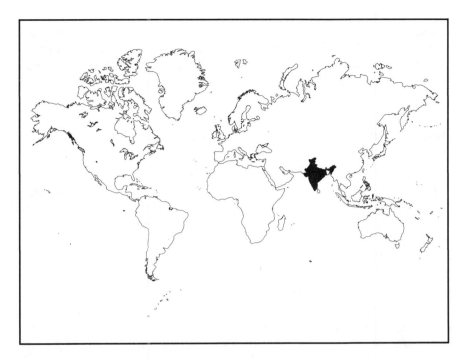

Experienced boundary crossers realize that there are certain protocols that ease cultural entrances and exits, behavioral routines that lessen stress on those with whom we interact in our comings and goings. As any actor or actress knows, making an entrance is a critical moment and can determine the manner in which the rest of the scene is played. It is also important to observe the theatrical protocol against "upstaging" the other players or "hogging the limelight." And then there are the exits. When do you accomplish them unobtrusively and when do you make them a "grand finale"? Accomplishing these arrivals and departures in a manner that improves *everyone's* performance has to do with simple— and not so simple—good manners, as the next example indicates.

## SAYING GOOD-BYE

Louise Kidder encountered an "exit problem" when she first arrived in India to commence a year's field work in social psychology. Neighbor wives would drop by for a protocol visit, and the visit would go on and on and on. It was clear to Kidder that the visitors wanted to leave, but they didn't. She did notice the wives making an odd movement of the head (they moved it toward their shoulder in a kind of a nervous jerk), but it did not mean anything to her.

### What happened?

Louise did not know how to bring the social calls to an end.

### What really happened?

The ritual cue that indicated a desire to end the visit, and the corresponding permission, were not effectively perceived by Louise. It was some weeks before she understood the meaning of the head jerk. The women were signaling that it was time to go and expected Kidder to agree by returning the same nonverbal signal.

### What can Louise do now?

Louise described the situation to some British friends, and they told her what the leave-taking custom was. She made a point of making her solicitous neighbors feel more comfortable with her by making many brief visits in the forthcoming days.

### How can this misunderstanding be avoided in the future?

In future similar encounters in cultures that are new to her, Louise (and the rest of us) will anticipate the existence of a ritual device for ending social calls. She may even, under similar circumstances, say something like, ''You are welcome to stay as long as you like, but I sense that you may want to get back to your home. But since I'm new to local customs, I don't know how you indicate this.''

Ned made a successful entry into a Shuar home in the upper-Amazon jungle by doing nothing at all, after a fashion. He had been invited for dinner with two other colleagues, both of whom were Shuar from other villages. (The Shuar are better known as the Jívaros of shrunken-head fame.) The four had been traveling together for weeks conducting a social survey. By the time they walked up the steps to their companion's log-and-branch home, Ned had learned the entry protocol: maintain complete silence until the host asks the guests a question. (Another Shuar variety of this protocol is for the host to initiate a singsong rhymed

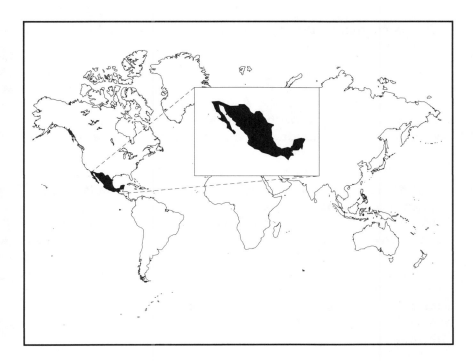

repartee with the guest. This can go on for twenty minutes or more. But to do this you have to be fluent in the Shuar language.)

Sometimes things simply aren't done the way they are back home. The next three examples provide variations of this theme.

## WHO MOWS THE GRASS?

A U.S. executive of a large brewery was sent to Mexico to oversee a start-up operation. He made arrangements to rent a beautiful house that had been vacant for some weeks. Noticing that weeds had intruded into the garden, he asked a local gardener how much he would charge to service the grounds. The executive later recounted to his friends that as soon as he heard the cost, he knew that the Mexican was taking advantage of him because he was a "rich American." "Well, I'll show them I

wasn't born yesterday. I'm buying a Weed-Eater to take back [to Mexico].
I'll mow my own damn lawn!''

# Analysis
## *What happened?*
A U.S. executive, angry that he was being asked an exorbitant price for
lawn and garden maintenance, decides to do the job himself.

## *What really happened?*
The U.S. executive failed to note the spirit of negotiation (also known
as price haggling) that is customary in much of Mexico. He could have
bargained a better price. It is worth noting, however, that his language
betrayed an ethnocentric distrust of Mexicans in general. He stereotyped
them. He didn't say "Well, I'll show *him* [the gardener] . . .''; he said
"I'll show *them* . . .'' As for being taken advantage of because he was
"a rich American,'' well he *was* a rich American. First, the average wages
paid to Americans is well above the average wages earned by Mexicans,
and second, he was earning well above the average earnings even for an
American.

## *What can the executive do now?*
If someone doesn't tell him, the executive will soon become the butt
of local ridicule for tending his own grounds, instead of contracting
manual work out to people who do that type of work. (Executives do
not do manual work in most highly hierarchical societies.) As a result,
establishing rapport in the community will be even more difficult than
it otherwise would be. The executive has to develop a little faith in
Mexicans in general and discover the local way of getting things done.

## *How can this misunderstanding be avoided in the future?*
One way to avoid problems is to check your stereotypes at the border.
Stereotypes pose an interesting paradox. Although often woefully out
of date or outrageously derogatory, they often capture characteristics that
are common in the target society (or at least more common than they
are "back home''). Why are they so insidious even when they generalize
accurately? The answer is that stereotypes lead us to ignore the considerable variety of personalities that make up any society.

L. Robert Kohls' popular booklet, *Survival Kit for Overseas Living*, lists a series of common descriptors of Americans: outgoing, friendly, informal, loud, boastful, hard-working, wasteful, confident they have all the answers, lacking in class consciousness, disrespectful of authority, ignorant of other countries, wealthy, generous, always in a hurry. Kohls then makes the point that to the extent an American fits the stereotypes, he or she will be likely to experience problems abroad, since even our "virtues" may be considered liabilities by another society. It is disconcerting for someone reared in a culture that values individualism to have someone abroad treat you as a "typical American." Conversely, our own stereotypes of other peoples can rob them of much of their richness as individuals.

Intimacy with a variety of people and in-depth knowledge of the institutions that help form their personalities are a powerful antidote to generalizations gone wild. Ask people questions concerning the *range* of behaviors observable in the target culture. Do not limit yourself to questions emphasizing central tendencies, because these generalizations can lead to stereotyping.

---

The next example illustrates how easily *you* can be stereotyped simply by not picking up on "minor" details.

# SOME—MAYBE ALL—OF YOUR BEST FRIENDS ARE SLOBS

Ray Gorden was in charge of overseeing the well-being of American exchange students who lived with Colombian hosts in Bogotá. Noticing that the hosts were forming unfavorable views of their American guests, Gorden sent Colombian interviewers to identify the precise behaviors that provoked the negative reaction. The interviewers reported back to Gorden that the Americans were, among other things, alienating their hosts through unkempt behavior. Gorden asked the interviewers what behaviors had offended the hosts. "They were dirty," they replied.

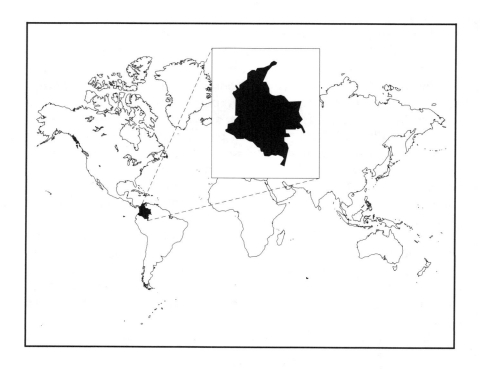

## Analysis
### *What happened?*

The American students did things that their Colombian hosts considered unpleasantly grubby and/or bawdy; there was some ambiguity in the interviewers' response.

### *What really happened?*

When Gorden questioned the interviewers more closely, he discovered that there were many such behaviors, but one in particular had the direst consequences: where the Americans put their towels after bathing. They put them everywhere except in the one acceptable place. They hung them over the towel rack or over the shower curtain. They dropped them in a corner on the floor; they put them in the dirty clothes hamper. They draped the towels over a chair in their bedroom. All these behaviors gave the Colombians evidence of the slovenly nature of the Americans, and as a result the guests were not invited on family outings and were marginalized during social events occurring within the home.

### What can Ray do now?

He quickly got the word out to the American guests. Where, you might ask, were they *supposed* to put the towel in the particular circumstances of the middle-class homes in the Bogotá of the day? Why, over a line in the patio to dry! It was a custom none of the Americans picked up on in the semester or two they lived in Bogotá.

### How can this misunderstanding be avoided in the future?

Gorden began to train the Americans to ask more questions about mundane behavior. Asking "stupid" questions often helps. But there's a right way and a wrong way to ask questions, he notes.

The questions you ask, to be effective in many cultures, have to be open-ended and/or indirect. If you want to 'wash some clothes out and want to know where, you don't ask whether it is all right to wash them in the tub or in the river or in the washing machine. You ask, first, if it is all right for you to wash some clothes or if it would be better to get your clothes cleaned some other way. If it is all right, you then ask where an appropriate place would be to wash them. One American student asked the *señora* whether it would be all right to wash out her clothes over there in the *pila* (a kind of cement washboard) in the kitchen area. The *señora* said yes, it would be all right, when in fact she didn't want the guest to wash her clothes there. (She wanted her to pay the maid a small sum to do it for her in the *pila* in the rear patio.) In many cultures, people will give you the answer it is obvious you want to hear. This is a way to extend a courtesy to the guest. But it strains relationships a bit. Asking the question indirectly might lead to a query such as, "It must be hard to keep your clothes clean in this climate."

You can ask the type of personal questions that you are being asked, but you should be leery of asking personal questions that you do not hear others asking. Sometimes simple questions such as What does your father do? or Where did you go to school? may cause some embarrassment because they are social-class markers. Other simple questions may encroach on the domain of "privileged" information. Two questions asked by a Saudi visitor to a startled stranger on a London tram come to mind: "How much did your house cost?" "How much do you earn?"

---

The next example shows the cross-cultural significance of a simple, nonverbal gesture—the smile.

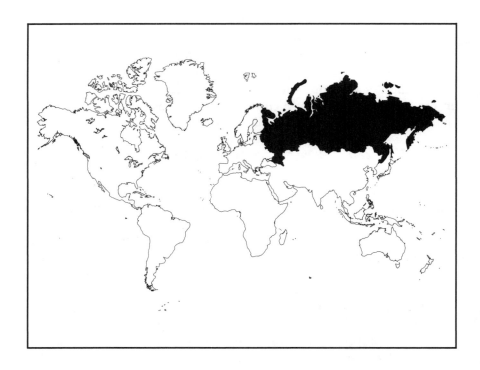

## TO MCSMILE OR NOT TO MCSMILE,
## THAT IS THE QUESTION

In 1990, McDonald's opened the first branch of its fast food restaurant in Russia, only a few blocks from Moscow's Kremlin. It was the largest McDonald's in the world and was well received by the do-it-on-a-grand-scale Russians—the 20,000 customers served that day broke McDonald's opening-day world record. A visiting corporate executive from company headquarters in Oak Brook, Illinois, was quite pleased but did notice, *because of its absence*, one of the hallmarks of his company's restaurants—the friendly employees. In their training programs, McDonald's stresses the importance of conveying friendliness by smiling at the customers when they take the orders. The Russian employees did not smile.

Making a note of this, the U.S. executive asked the person in charge of training about this.

# Analysis

### *What happened?*

Contrary to standard operating procedures in the training guidelines, the Russian employees of McDonald's did not smile at the customers as they took their orders.

### *What really happened?*

The level of established rapport often can be measured through nonverbal communication, such as smiles. Nonverbal communication, however, is culture-specific and there are many cases in which the same nonverbal sign can be interpreted differently, depending on the culture. In this case, Russians do not customarily smile at strangers. They do not show hostility or disrespect, but they do not smile. You smile at someone you know. Smiling at strangers would show an inappropriate amount of familiarity.

### *What can McDonald's do now?*

In the course of the training program, the U.S. trainers noticed the reluctance of the Russian trainees to smile at strangers, asked about it, and found other forms of behavior which made McDonald's an inviting place to eat (quick service in a clean, pleasantly designed establishment).

### *How can this misunderstanding be avoided in the future?*

Most problems such as this one you learn through trial and error. The more experienced you become at intercultural communication, the less you take for granted. You become more adept at asking questions.

---

The next account also takes place in Russia and it too deals with pleasantries.

---

# IT'S A PLEASURE TO MEET YOU, BUDDY

---

Alexander Supikov, raised in Chicago in a Russian-speaking home, was visiting relatives in Russia when he was introduced to an important business

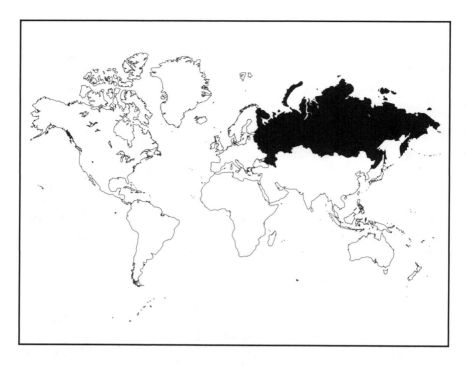

contact (someone not related to Alexander). Alexander used his knowledge of Russian to greet the older man. The man seemed taken aback somewhat by Alexander's greeting. Alexander ascribed this to his surprise in hearing an American speak Russian. Over the course of the conversation, the older man mostly frowned; several times the man seemed to wince. Alexander sensed the level of discomfort in the man, but he could not understand why. Perhaps, thought Alexander, he is in ill health.

### *What happened?*
The older man didn't like Alexander, or maybe Alexander did or said the wrong thing.

### *What really happened?*
What in fact happened was that Alexander had innocently used the familiar form of the word *you* in the greeting and in the subsequent conversation. While many languages make this distinction, English does not differentiate formal and informal verb inflections. Alexander should have used the formal form *Bbl* rather than *Tbl*. In Russian culture this

connotes respect and formality. Since Alexander spoke with a certain level of fluency and had a Russian surname, the contact was offended when Alex referred to him in the informal form. The formal address should not be dropped until the other party grants permission. If Alexander had had an American accent and surname, he might have gotten away with his error, but often language fluency is taken to mean similar cultural upbringing.

### What can Alexander do now?

Alexander had to work to recover from this faux pas in order to rebuild confidence and trust. In this case, he didn't know what had caused the distressed reaction from his Russian contact. He did the right thing in asking a Russian colleague how his approach might have caused discomfort. From then on Alexander spoke to strangers, older people, and superiors in the *Bbl* form.

### How can this misunderstanding be avoided in the future?

A good rule to use is that if you are in doubt, use the formal form until you are otherwise advised. People who learn the host language in informal situations (at home, with a boy or girl friend, or on the street) need to be especially alert to this. It is commonplace for a language to have distinct pronouns and verb forms to recognize social class differences. One society in Africa even has a distinct form of address to differentiate boys who have not yet been circumcised!

---

An experience that happened to a manager who worked with clients from many countries illustrates another rule—the proper way of eating.

# PIGS FLY AND YOU HAVE A SECOND CHANCE TO MAKE A FIRST IMPRESSION

Marie-Antoinette, a quality control manager based in Paris, was invited to dine at the Saudi Embassy with her Muslim clients when she discovered

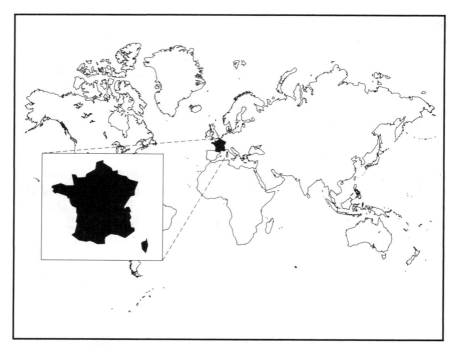

she had an unanticipated liability. An enormous plate of rice and lamb was placed in the center of the table. With considerable enthusiasm, she picked food from various parts of the plate. She was left-handed.

Marie-Antoinette noticed that her hosts, while remaining polite, became less talkative. They did not appear to be very hungry. She thought that perhaps they had eaten a late lunch; that would explain their loss of appetite.

## Analysis
### *What happened?*
Marie-Antoinette's Muslim hosts did not seem to enjoy her company.

### *What really happened?*
A colleague later filled her in on her faux pas, as it were. The left hand does not go into the communal food repository because the left hand is used for personal toilet hygiene in Islamic countries.

### *What can Marie-Antoinette do now?*
Apologize.

### *How can this misunderstanding be avoided in the future?*

Table etiquette and social graces are tied to one's cultural upbringing. There is a path you can follow when you find yourself in these situations: take time to observe how the others present are behaving—and follow their lead.

Had Marie-Antoinette been warned ahead of time, she might have noticed that all the others were eating with their right hand and only picking from the food that was directly in front of them on the table. Had she taken the time to read up on their social customs she might not have erred.

---

For those who regularly travel from country to country, you might not have the opportunity to read up on social customs. At some point you will be put in a situation in which what you normally do will get you into trouble. General rules, such as observing before acting, may save you from some grief and discomfort.

Ray Gorden advises that the key to learning how to function effectively in another culture is to learn the discrete behavioral patterns that are employed there. His masterful book, *Living in Latin America: A Case Study in Cross-Cultural Communication*, answers the question of just how this learning is to occur. It occurs when the right questions are asked in the right way. A reading of Gorden's book goes a long way toward alerting us to the fact that each culture has its own space and role requirements.

Simply being aware that there are magic rituals that facilitate rapport and that there are cryptic turn-offs that discourage friendships will help you establish satisfying relationships.

## TOOLBOX
# Unpredictable Turn-Offs

- Always assume that there are microbehaviors associated with all areas of interaction that may be critical to establishing rapport.

- Read up on local customs before you arrive. Once you are in the culture, ask about the *specific* things you are expected to do *and* which behaviors you are to avoid.

- When people's reactions suggest that you may have done or said the wrong thing, ask whether you have unintentionally stuck your foot in your mouth.

# 8

# Your (Negotiating) Style or Mine?

Four examples illustrate the pitfalls of intercultural persuasion and negotiation. The first looks at gender and subcultural differences in how you go about initiating "negotiations" in matters of interpersonal relationships. The second illustrates that a rose is not a rose and that you have to plead your case within accepted principles. In the third example, interest in a project hinged on the absence of a single word. Finally, *who* you negotiate with is at least as critical as *how* you negotiate. There are at least a dozen things to take into consideration before, during, and after international negotiations, and these provide a checklist for negotiators to fill in before getting on the airplane.

## Reaching an Agreement

You have an effective communication strategy and you have established rapport with the people with whom you will work. So far, so good. You are being paid, however, to get things done. This chapter (and the following two) examines the fine art of persuasion.

How you negotiate an agreement depends on where you are and with whom you are negotiating. Courtship rituals quickly illustrate how *where* you are affects negotiations. In some Western cultures it boils down to one line: "Your place or mine?" In rural Bolivia, young Aymara Indian women show their interest in a suitor by throwing stones at him. Even today, in a few small-town plazas in Mexico on Sunday afternoons there is a public ritual that allows both genders a chance to look each other over—under the conservative eyes of relatives: the males circle the gazebo in one direction, and the females circle in the opposite direction. When the male fancies a lass, he pauses as they meet and gives her a rose or a carnation. If she is *not* interested in him, she accepts the flower with a *gracias*. If she *is* interested in the lad, she smiles coquettishly but refuses the flower. This she repeats the next time, a few minutes later, when he offers her another flower. On the third attempt, she accepts the flower. This encourages the lad to begin a highly stylized (and highly supervised) courtship, beginning with a visit to the girl's home.

But all is not harmonious in dreamland. When young men and women from different cultures meet at the village gazebo or in the workplace, toes get stepped on. One U.S. woman's patience was sorely tried in her New York City neighborhood, where in good weather increasing numbers of Puerto Ricans would congregate on their doorsteps, people-watching. Some would say things to her as she passed, things in Spanish she thought were "obscene," although she did not know the language. Within a Hispanic context, these commonplace *piropos* generally are not obscene. Some are absurdly poetic: "Would that your lips were an airplane and mine a landing field. . . ." Still, to that woman, ignorant of accepted Hispanic cultural forms, they were threatening. Hispanic women simply ignore them most of the time. Occasionally, if the *piropo* is especially poetic or humorous, she might smile discreetly.

In a multicultural world, foreign countries are not the only places where one finds cultural misunderstandings. The diversity of our workforce ensures that workers who have internalized different assumptions, beliefs, and values will occasionally misunderstand each other. Canada, like most countries, is made up of many subcultures, each distinct in its own way. Gender and ethnic or racial differences abound, as the next account illustrates.

# ME TARZAN, YOU JANE

In a cardboard box factory in Toronto, about half of the workforce was made up of immigrants, mostly from the Commonwealth nations. About sixty percent were women.

One day, Mabel, an attractive Canadian-born woman, left the floor on her break to go outside for a smoke. As she passed four or five West Indian men in shipping, one of them said to her: "Hey, baby, I like what I see. I bet you got some great movements." Ignoring him, Mabel continued on her way. In a louder voice, the male admirer, looking at

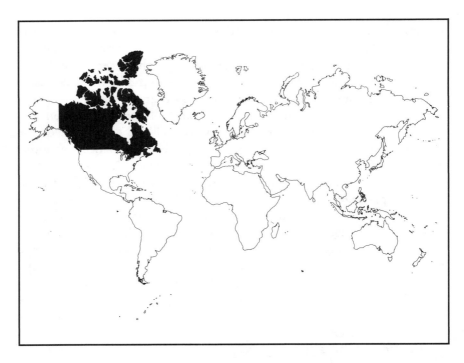

her bottom, said: "Shake it, baby." Charles, the admirer, walked over to her and placed his hand on her arm to guide her away from the group where they could talk more privately. At this point, Mabel wrenched around and shouted, "Leave me alone, goddamnit!"

Upset, Mabel filed a sexual harassment grievance with her supervisor. The culprit, Charles, was called into the office, explained the charges, and suspended for three days without pay. "Hell, all I did was tell her she looked great," said the suspended worker.

## Analysis
### What happened?

A man sexually harassed a woman at work and was suspended. This touches on perhaps the main point of contention between the genders as they share the same workplace, and it occurs in the boardroom as well as on the factory floor.

### What really happened?

The West Indian's approach to the woman might not have been considered either obscene, threatening, or inappropriate by some of the West

Indian women working at the plant. Men are expected to make verbal overtures to women, and the latter will sometimes "grade" the males' "rap." Charles kept getting louder because Mabel was ignoring him. While working-class males in the West Indies tend to assume that women are *generally* sexually interested people, they do not assume that any *specific* woman will be interested in any specific man at any given time. In white English-speaking circles in Canada and the United States, it is more prevalent to hold the belief that men are potential aggressors who must hold themselves in check to protect women who, by disposition, are only passive sexual beings. An approach Canadian women do not usually object to would be one that pretends that sex has nothing to do with it. Instead, an interested male might pose an "innocent" question; physical attractiveness (i.e., sex) would not be overtly mentioned. "Are you a hockey fan?" might be a safer beginning. Mabel's frightened and angry reaction to what she regarded as a boundary violation surprised Charles.

### What can management do now to make both genders more comfortable?

What management often does is to ignore the issue and hope that it will go away, or to impose—loudly and clearly—a list of behaviors that are unacceptable in the workplace. The underlying assumptions of this list generally reflect the middle-class female views of what is proper and improper behavior. The result is that the new rules of behavior are communicated to everyone and "threatening" and "obscene" behavior diminishes. One cost of this approach is that males, especially those who belong to a minority culture, are sometimes resentful. Tough cookies!, many harassed women might say.

### How can this misunderstanding be avoided in the future?

Sexual harassment is not always—or even mostly—a matter of differences in cultural styles, and both women and men need to be protected from exploitation with clear guidelines and just enforcement of them. However, when the workforce knows the different approach styles that are common in other cultures—cultures that are represented in one's work and neighborhood settings—this knowledge may provide a bit of a buffer separating cross-culturally "inappropriate" behavior from demeaning or threatening behavior. Still, men will have to become more sensitive to the growing sense of outrage that women feel as a result of disrespectful interplay with "dominant" males in many of the world's cultures.

Worldwide demographics reveal a significant increase in the diversity of the workplace. In the United States, there are estimates that by the year 2000, 85 percent of the new jobs created will be held by women, people of color, and immigrants. Urban centers throughout the world are experiencing similar trends.

Throughout the globe, the negotiating process differs no matter what you are negotiating. Sarah Lubman, writing in *The Wall Street Journal* (Dec. 10, 1993, p. R3) describes an experience Henry Kissinger had in China. Kissinger was negotiating a communiqué in Beijing. The Chinese negotiating team kept him on edge the entire visit. Avoiding negotiations, they stalled for hours. Kissinger set a deadline for conclusion of the negotiations. Finally, at midnight before the self-imposed deadline, he was presented with an unacceptable contract. The lesson here is to avoid subjecting yourself to specific deadlines.

Your company's profits depend on negotiating a reasonable contract. Since the process for doing this varies from country to country, how, then, do you find out how to negotiate in new markets? What can you do to minimize unpleasant surprises?

Pierre Casse describes four general negotiation styles: *factual* ("The facts speak for themselves"), *intuitive* ("Imagination can solve any problem"), *normative* ("Negotiating is bargaining"), and *analytical* ("Logic leads to the right conclusion"). (An elaboration of this appears in Casse and Deol, and in Moran and Harris; both sources include the following guidelines for negotiating with people having styles that differ from your own.)

---

| TOOLBOX |

# Guidelines for Negotiating with People Having Different Styles

1. Negotiating with someone having a *factual* style:
   - Be precise in presenting your facts.
   - Refer to the past (which has already been tried out, what has worked, what has been shown from past experiences . . .).
   - Be inductive (go from the facts to the principles).
   - Know your dossier (including the details).
   - Document what you say.

2. Negotiating with someone having an *intuitive* style:
   - Focus on the situation as a whole.
   - Project yourself into the future (look for opportunities).
   - Tap the imagination and creativity of your partner.
   - Be quick in reacting (jump from one idea to another).
   - Build upon the reaction of the other person.

3. Negotiating with someone having an *analytical* style:
   - Use logic when arguing.
   - Look for causes and effects.
   - Analyze the relationships between the various elements of the situation or problem at stake.
   - Be patient.
   - Analyze various options with their respective pros and cons.

4. Negotiating with someone having a *normative* style:
   - Establish a sound relationship right at the outset of the negotiation.
   - Show your interest in what the other person is saying.
   - Identify his or her values and adjust to them accordingly.
   - Be ready to compromise.
   - Appeal to your partner's feelings.

How do you learn the applicable negotiating styles before you go to the table?

There is a simple methodology, and preparation is the key to it. Although there is no crystal ball to foresee all obstacles, the twelve-point framework for global negotiations developed by Robert T. Moran and William G. Stripp provides an especially useful checklist of issues you need to research prior to negotiating in a country in which you lack experience.

## How Do You Find Answers?

There are basically two sources: other people or library resources. Other people may include a veteran negotiator with experience in the target country or a consultant firm specialized in preparing negotiators for a specific country. When you arrive at your destination, most embassies have commercial attaches or economic officers who may be able to give you an overview of local negotiation styles; they will be able to introduce

# Moran & Stripp's Twelve Critical Variables in Negotiating Cross-Culturally

This checklist provides the basic methodological frame for preparing for cross-cultural negotiations. Conscious effort should be directed at understanding the dynamics of each of these twelve elements in the target business culture prior to entering into formal negotiations. Where does the host country team fall on each of these critical variables? Where does your team fall?

1. Basic concept of negotiation:
   strategic _____ synergistic

2. Selection of negotiators:
   technical ability _____ social skills

3. Role of individual aspirations:
   organization _____ self

4. Concern with protocol:
   formal _____ informal

5. Significance of type of issue:
   substantive _____ relationship-based

6. Complexity of language:
   verbal _____ nonverbal

7. Nature of persuasive argument:
   logic _____ emotion

8. Value of time:
   strict _____ relaxed

9. Basis of trust:
   law _____ friendship

10. Risk-taking propensity:
    cautious _____ adventurous

11. Internal decision-making systems:
    authoritative _____ consensus

12. Form of satisfactory agreement:
    explicit _____ implicit

you to local business people. One valuable library source for developing marketing plans is the *National Trade Data Bank* on CD ROM disks(updated monthly). It is prepared by the U.S. Department of Commerce, alphabetized by country, and indexed by product. Every U.S. depository library has the data bank.

In what way should you adjust your strategy after you have gone through this exercise? In Nigeria a deal is closed with a verbal agreement. Two thousand miles north, the Germans conclude a deal with a written contract that leaves no room for ambiguity. When negotiating in Germany, the value of time will be very strict, more so than in the United States. Do not arrive ten to fifteen minutes late; this will not go over well. In South Korea, the custom is to haggle over cost. Consequently, when negotiating, the Koreans' opening price tends to be much higher than what they will settle for. And so on through the planet's many nations.

In the next account, the paradoxical presence of negotiating flexibility led to a tearful scene.

# FLEXIBILITY IS (OR IS NOT) THE KEY

Rose Kong, a talented young Chinese-Malaysian woman enrolled in a master's program at a university in Tokyo, encountered little difficulty working with her thesis committee. Committee members were reasonable and flexible in helping Rose deal with the exigencies that arose over the course of the year she worked on the thesis. The thesis was due, she was told, by 4:30 P.M. on the tenth of January. A hard-working, conscientious student, Rose saw the completion date as tight but doable. After making last-minute editing and formatting touch-ups on her word processor, Rose began running off a draft of the completed thesis on her dot matrix printer the afternoon before it was due. Inevitably, some formatting problems came to her attention, and she fixed them. She would print the final copy the next day on a laser printer at the university's Computer Center.

Early the next morning she went to the Computer Center and encountered a series of difficulties. All of the machines were in use; two undergraduate professors had assigned term papers due that day.

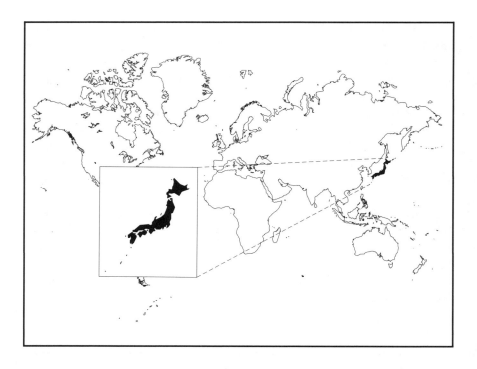

After considerable delay, a printer became available, but it was low on toner and wouldn't print acceptably legible copy. Extra toner was locked in a cabinet and no one could find the key. Several hours were lost tracking down the lab assistant who could open the cabinet. By now it was early afternoon. There was still enough time to print the thesis. Everything was going along fine until the printer reached the bibliography at the end of the thesis. For some reason known only to cyberspace, it found the bibliography undigestible, promptly recorded a technical glitch, and froze. No one could get the printer to work. She looked at the clock. It was 4:00 P.M. Rose took the final version of her thesis—minus the bibliography— rushed back to her dorm, retrieved a dot-matrix copy of the bibliography, added it to her thesis, and ran to the dean's office to hand in the thesis. She arrived thirty minutes late.

She explained what had happened, including the temporary presence of a draft version of the bibliography. The dean refused to accept the thesis because it was late and incomplete at that. The deadline, he explained, had been clearly announced and was irrevocable. Rose calmly drew his attention to two other students within the past three years who had been granted extensions on their thesis due dates. The dean was inflexible. Rose, maintaining her professional demeanor, asked how the problem could be resolved. It could not be resolved, she was told. She would have to wait a year and meet next year's deadline (and pay another year's tuition).

# Analysis
## *What happened?*
Rose handed in her thesis late, and the dean wouldn't listen to reason. He would not accept the thesis.

## *What really happened?*
Rose assumed that the same atmosphere of flexibility that had attended her thesis development would apply to the due date. The school authorities, on the other hand, held start and finish dates as sacrosanct. In between these two dates, reasonable flexibility ruled.

## *What can Rose do now?*
Her approach to trying reasonable persuasion did not succeed. Rose based her case on an objective explanation of the last-minute unexpected mishaps in the Computer Center and on arguing precedents. In spite of her eloquence, her master's program was going down the tubes fast.
Rose was distraught, but there was no recourse.

## *How can this situation be avoided in the future?*
It is considered bad form to argue based on the fact that "so and so" was allowed to do it. Instead of arguing her case objectively, Rose should have thrown herself on the mercy of the court, so to speak. Emotionally pleading her case, mentioning the dishonor to her parents and grandparents, the tragedy to her life, and so on, might have evoked better results. But this situation concerned a non-negotiable requirement that was not tractable to persuasion. Several years previously, three undergraduate students at the same university had their senior theses destroyed in an earthquake. They asked permission to hand the papers in late. If this could not be arranged, the jobs that were waiting for them at graduation would vanish, and this would be a black mark on their careers for the

rest of their lives. A full faculty meeting was called to discuss the issue. The faculty voted to give them an extension, but denied them the right to graduate with the rest of their class. They obtained their degree a month later.

How do you tell whether a rule that appears inflexible is really negotiable? It's not an easy matter; experience is a harsh teacher. You have to observe and ask others; use their experience.

---

In the next account, a consultant has the task of finding out whether the Ministry of Education has any interest in a particular innovation aimed at rural children. If interest were discerned, then the consultant was to negotiate reasonable terms with the Ministry officials, draft a contract, and get both the Ministry and the funding source to agree to the details of a ten-year, multimillion-dollar pilot project.

## FINDING A HOME FOR AN ORPHAN INNOVATION

An international donor agency was interested in increasing the efficiency of the rural education system in Guatemala, where the majority of the students are Mayan Indian children who do not understand Spanish. The resources it takes to get a student through sixth grade primary school is substantial, since only five percent of the students who enroll in first grade ever graduate from sixth grade. The agency wanted to know whether the Ministry of Education would be willing to launch an experimental program taught in a Mayan language. Ned was contracted to find this out.

Ned visited a handful of officials in various divisions of the Ministry and simply asked them what they thought of the idea of bilingual education for Mayan Indian children. This was a direct, economic way to find out—the direct plan approach. It did not take the consultant long to discover that the idea of bilingual education was regarded as a terrible idea insofar as it involved indigenous languages. Ironically, bilingual education was quite popular in private urban schools where the elite send their children to learn English or French or German. Not a single

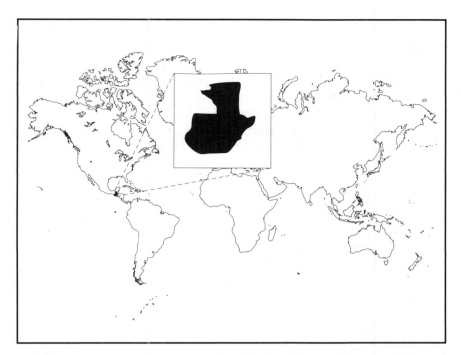

middle or upper manager approached in the Ministry thought bilingual education in indigenous languages for rural students was worth considering. Worse, the very term *bilingual education* was anathema to them. There were many reasons for this. It had not been done before in Guatemalan public schools. There was a strong feeling that Indian children should assimilate quickly, and the best way to do that was to immerse them in Spanish (although only half of the school-aged children enrolled, and half of them flunked out of first grade). There were few teachers capable or willing to teach in a Mayan language. Indian languages did not have the prestige that European languages enjoyed.

The concept of using indigenous languages as an aid in public primary school education appeared to Ned to have merit notwithstanding the Ministry's objections. What to do? One thing was clear. Whatever the innovation was called, it could not be called "bilingual education." The consultant searched the national Code of Education for any legal helps or hindrances. He found an auspicious passage that talked about providing rural education for indigenous children in ways that were "appropriate for the setting." There were no legal obstacles to using indigenous languages to teach in public schools.

Ned searched throughout the Ministry looking for an established department that might provide fertile grounds to grow a bilingual program, in concept if not in name. He looked for some place where there was a concentration of indigenous Mayan-speaking professionals. He found a propitious place in an obscure department that provided a transitional preschool program for rural Mayan-speaking children. The program taught Spanish as a second language while it prepared the children to handle the academic concepts of first grade by instructing them through their native language—the only one they understood. They called the program "preschool *castellanización*" (the Spanish conceptual equivalent of an "Americanization" program for immigrants). The professionals involved in this program had received a dispensation from the Ministry: they only needed to have a sixth-grade primary school education and to be bilingual in Spanish and a Mayan language. Although these professionals did not enjoy the prestige of more credentialed members of the Ministry, they did have the sensitivity that was a prerequisite for developing curriculum for Mayan Indian children, and they had the beginning of a program that could extend into the primary grades.

After discussing their program for some weeks with these professionals—without using the term *bilingual education*—Ned asked them if there were any need to expand, or otherwise improve, the program. There were, of course, areas in which they saw the need for improvement. The consultant called the proposed amorphous intervention "Project for the Improvement of the National Preschool Castellanización Program." This unwieldy title was accepted by Ministry personnel without objection.

The proposed "improvements" included continuing Spanish as a second language and vernacular-language education through the second or third grade in four Mayan languages that two-thirds of indigenous Guatemalans spoke. A task force composed of representatives of a half dozen Ministry departments was formed by the Vice Minister to plan the details of the "improved preschool program." Many of the appointees were department heads; Ned was appointed a member of this group as an outside consultant.

About a year into the task force deliberations, one of the members stumbled over the title *El Proyecto para el Mejoramiento del Programa Nacional Pre-escolar de Castellanización* and exclaimed, "There must be a better title for this project!" In the brief discussion that followed, one of the team members (not the consultant) said, "Why don't we call it 'Bilingual Education Program?'" It was quickly agreed by all in attendance that this was both easier to say and more descriptive of the project. It had taken a year to get used to the idea (membership on the task force varied from time to time due to political changes). After the prestigious task force had become quite interested in the project and had consecrated the term *bilingual education*, there were no further objections raised in Ministry circles, and the negotiations returned to outlining the details of the project.

# Analysis
## *What happened?*
The consultant discovered in the first two weeks of his consultancy that no one in Guatemala approved of "bilingual education." Since he was charged with finding out whether there was any interest by Ministry officials in bilingual education, he could have reported back to the donor agency that indeed, no, there was no interest.

## *What really happened?*
The consultant thought that it might have been the term more than the concept that turned off the Ministry officials, although he found no initial support for the concept, either, beyond a one-year transitional preschool education for rural Indians.

Being direct is not an efficient way to open negotiations for many— maybe even most—people outside the United States. Putting key information up front may lead your counterpart to believe that such information represents only a starting point from which to bargain. Typically, one is expected to refuse the first offer one receives, and although this was not the case in this study, there still is a tendency in many cultures for people to immediately reject new ideas until they have considered them and given them their own spin.

## *What can the consultant do now?*
Once he discovered the term *bilingual education* to be anathema, he stopped using it. He quickly dropped the "direct plan approach" and, instead, began describing the proposed innovation in very general terms. Meanwhile, he searched for someplace within the Ministry where the innovation might find a better reception, and for new ways to sell the idea. He hung his hat on the one area of the Ministry of Education where the concept of bilingual education was accepted—the preschool

*castellanización* programs. He asked the staff who worked in that program about their ideas on how to improve the preschool *castellanización* programs. Relying on the sensitivity of the Mayan-speaking Indians who staffed that department to be willing to move in sound directions, the consultant suggested basing the new project there.

### *How can this misunderstanding be avoided in the future?*

In countries or situations that do not regard time as money, a more exploratory approach may prove more efficient than getting right to the point. This is especially true in situations in which you do not know the buzz words.

---

In the next account, negotiations that had gone on for two years were not progressing well.

## MISAPPRAISAL OF THE COUNTERPART TEAM

Scott, a high-powered wheeler-dealer, had developed a creative plan for modernizing the tool and die industry in the Ukraine. Through consolidating the existing facilities and capital expenditures on state-of-the-art machinery, the industry could get back on track. While helping the Ukraine considerably, the project would bring in substantial fees to Scott's firm.

Scott was working with a group from New York in getting the needed support for the ambitious undertaking. Scott made a preliminary visit to the Ukraine to identify those governmental officials who were most knowledgeable about the tool and die industry and who were potentially interested in modernizing the industry. Scott found people who met these criteria in middle management positions. Preliminary talks went well, and Scott returned to New York with a list of the names of the officials who met both criteria; he had talked to them all. Scott got the go-ahead from his New York backers to initiate formal negotiations. Considerable time and money were spent persuading the tool and die specialists within the Ukraine

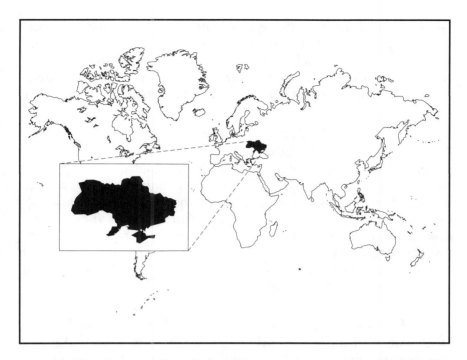

government of the benefits of the approach. After more than twenty-four months of hard work and hefty expenses, it did not seem that Scott and his venture capitalist friends were any closer to closing the deal in spite of the favorable reception by the Ukraine officials.

## Analysis
### *What happened?*

Managers in Scott's firm working together with "can-do" venture capitalists spent over two years and lots of money trying to build support for this ambitious program. After all the time and money, there was still no signed contract to show for their efforts.

### *What really happened?*

The team had in fact developed support for the program with the middle-level members of government whom they approached. However, they had failed to take into account the limited decision-making authority of the middle managers. In this highly hierarchical government setting, high-level decisions were not delegated to middle members. Scott's two-pronged criteria for identifying government officials—knowledge and interest—omitted a crucial third criterion—authorization to make contract decisions. The most knowledgeable officials were mid-level technicians, while the ones with decision-making authority were upper managers; both should have participated in the negotiations.

### *What can Scott do now?*

The team needs to decide how important it is to break into this former Soviet market and determine how much time and how many dollar resources it is willing to allot in obtaining the contract. If there are still resources the team can set aside to deal with the actual decision-maker(s), then two determinations can be made: first, whether the decision-maker(s) support the program or whether they can be persuaded to support the program, and second, whether there are sufficient resources for financing the program, including contingencies that may need to be overcome for a successful implementation.

### *How can this frustration be avoided in the future?*

Don't assume that decision-making follows the same lines as the ones you are accustomed to. Find out how the decision-making process works in the host country. If you don't know how it works, ask someone who does. When this is clear, change your negotiation strategy to one that will work in the host environment. This strategy should identify who needs to be persuaded to do what and how this will be accomplished. Tasks can then be prioritized and time and money resources allocated. In other words, don't spend all your time and money building sponsorship in low-level players that may have no influence on the final decision.

In the example from Guatemala, the consultant began his discussions with people in low levels of the Ministry of Education, but once he had a sense of the buzz words of negotiation in that site and of the general parameters of the project that might be acceptable, he moved the negotiations to upper and middle managers appointed by a top official. (This still could have fallen through if the top official had not delegated sufficient authority.)

How do you learn if the actual decision-maker is on the negotiating team? The answer to this question may alter how (and when and where) your financial and personnel resources will be deployed. A contact within the organization may provide a lead. Other sources include research on the country, businesspersons and/or consultants who work in the host country, and the local embassy.

In the Ukraine story the nature of the internal decision-making system, a critical variable, was not taken into consideration by the U.S. firm, and it cost them a contract. In the Guatemalan study, the consultant discovered that language issues—buzz words—were about to undermine his efforts. Both these issues are included in Moran & Stripp's twelve-point framework for global negotiations, outlined in the Toolbox on page 130.

---

Good advice is offered by Lennie Copeland and Lewis Griggs.

| TOOLBOX |

# Copeland & Griggs' Twenty Practical Rules for International Negotiations

### Before the Negotiations

Rule 1: Make sure what you are negotiating is negotiable.

Rule 2: Define what "winning" the negotiation means to you. Be ambitious but set a realistic walk-away.

Rule 3: Get the facts.

Rule 4: Have a strategy for each culture and each phase. First, decide how to position your proposal. Second, decide whether to be competitive (win-lose) or cooperative (win-win). Third, set your opening offer. Fourth, plan to control your concessions.

Rule 5: Send a winning team. Don't go alone. Always have your own interpreter. Exclude lawyers and accountants from the negotiating team. In some cases use a go-between.

Rule 6: Allow yourself plenty of time, and more. Never tell the other side when you are leaving.

### Beginning the Negotiations

Rule 7: Make the opening scene work for you. Think about the agenda. Watch the physical arrangements. The overture should make music.

## Hard Bargaining

Rule  8:   Control information.

Rule  9:   Watch your language.

Rule 10:   Persuasion is an art. Don't paint your argument with the wrong materials. Thinking on the same plane is important. Be wary of the persuasion strategies Americans love.

Rule 11:   Get in stride with the locals. Most important: take time out.

Rule 12:   Go behind the scenes—that is where minds are changed.

Rule 13:   Give face.

Rule 14:   A deadlock means neither side wins, but both may lose.

Rule 15:   Don't be browbeaten into a bad deal. You must be able to walk away.

Rule 16:   Get your agreement signed before you leave.

Rule 17:   Both sides should agree on the significance of what you are signing.

Rule 18:   Be willing to give up cherished notions of the proper contract.

## Beyond the Contract

Rule 19:   Discussions are always preferable to court settlements.

Rule 20:   Remember—without a relationship, you have no deal.

# 9

# Analysis without Paralysis

Knowing your market and your workforce is essential to successful project planning. You have melded your ideas with those of your local counterparts and negotiated a contract that serves both interests. Most projects begin with a planning phase. There are two common problems with this phase: making the planning practical (including taking cross-cultural contingencies into consideration), and paradoxically, *ending* the planning phase. Analysis paralysis is, alas, a common virus. And it can be fatal.

## Analysis

Before the paralysis, you have creeping analysis. You analyze because poorly planned ventures are costly, take longer to complete, and risk failure more than better planned ventures. This should not come as a surprise to anyone. You have to plan, but the trick is to avoid getting too much of a good thing. This results in paralysis.

Before examining the danger of planning paralysis, let us look at some examples of sound planning ideas that were not brought to the drawing board.

First, who is going to buy your product or service? You have to know your market—and sometimes it is fickle. A plant in former East Germany went to great effort and cost, after unification with the Bohn government, to update its machinery and retrain its personnel—only to discover that few consumers would buy what they considered to be an out-of-fashion coat. A U.S. company, after going to considerable lengths to break into the Japanese market, could not sell its refrigerators because they were too big for Japanese kitchens—apartments often

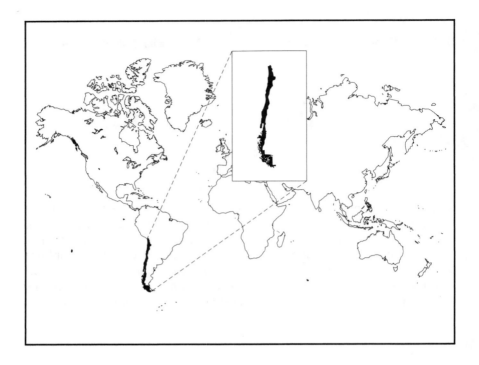

have only one square meter of walking space in their tiny kitchens. Furthermore, the refrigerators were too noisy for the paper-walled Japanese homes. Tupperware, on the other hand, sold well in Japan, not because of the advertised preservative quality of the product, but because of the need for economical storage containers that fit inside one another.

U.S. auto manufacturers publicly complained to the President of the United States that the Japanese market for their products was closed to them. Closer investigation revealed that the U.S. companies had not even bothered to put the steering wheel on the right-hand side of the car for a country that follows the same traffic patterns as the United Kingdom and 51 other countries. None of the effort expended in project implementation will amount to anything if the market has not been plumbed.

In the next example, a U.S. firm shot itself in the foot by ignoring a tool that is prevalent in many overseas markets—media ratings. The firm erroneously assumed it was entering an unsophisticated market without media ratings surveys.

# A CHILLY RECEPTION

One west-coast U.S. company wanted to introduce its product into South America. The product was aimed at adults between the ages of 24 and 38. The company arranged to have one-minute ads placed on three radio stations in Santiago, Chile. Listeners were invited to write in for a free book or record. A market research firm with experience in South America was called in at that point to measure listener response. In the face of very detailed evaluation specifications outlined by the client company, the research firm suggested that a more modest evaluation design might be more appropriate. "Things never go the way you plan in Latin America," the agency's head researcher told the west-coast company.

Hank arrived in Santiago several weeks after the initiation of the ad campaign to discover that there had been no response at all. Not a single listener had requested the free fulfillment!

## Analysis
### *What happened?*

The ad campaign was a total failure. Not a single listener had responded to the radio ads.

### *What really happened?*

The only clue was that the local person charged with monitoring the ads had only succeeded in locating the ads on one of the three target stations at the scheduled times. Still, even with one of the three radio stations airing the ads, there should have been some respondents.

### *What can Hank do now?*

Rather than return straightaway to the United States to give the bad news to the company that paid for the advertising, Hank began to look into the reason for the disastrous ad campaign. Through a friend of a friend he located a Chilean who worked in a local ad agency and talked the situation over with her. She lent Hank a copy of a recent radio ratings study which listed the audience, by age and gender, for every radio station in the country, by fifteen-minute segments. The client company had assumed there wouldn't be any ratings study in Chile—an assumption they would not have made in a U.S. or European setting.

Here Hank discovered that one of the three target radio stations catered to teenagers (not the target audience for the ad campaign) and another station did draw young adults but not at the particular hour that the ads were broadcast. The third station was an appropriate one to reach the desired audience at most any time, but that station had not broadcast any of the commercials!

Hank cabled the U.S. company and, because necks were on the chopping block, discreetly and diplomatically outlined what had happened and suggested different hours for the one station and identified other substitute stations for future airing. These changes were approved within the hour and were made within several days. The ads pulled, and Hank was then able to evaluate the effectiveness of the ad campaign. By that time, however, time and budget constraints precluded the tracking of many of the variables that had interested the client company's research department. Still, the evaluation report had positive findings to report and was well received.

### How can this situation be avoided in the future?

The selection of the original three stations was done by people who had not consulted the Santiago ratings; indeed, they were unaware that there were ratings for Santiago's radio stations. It is difficult to keep your hands on the pulse of a local ad campaign if your hands are a continent or so away from the action. A company representative in Santiago was asked to ascertain whether the ads were being aired, but the representative already had a full schedule. She tried to tune into the stations at the predetermined times but only succeeded in hearing the ads on one station. She was not authorized to deal with the stations face-to-face, so she did not take corrective action.

It was a learning experience, as they say. It would have been a disaster if Hank had not spoken Spanish and known his way around the block in Latin America.

---

On another front, to calculate manufacturing break-even levels for plant start-ups, you need to know the cost of capital investments, marketing costs, and the cost per unit of product. This last component of the equation can be tricky to estimate if you don't know the workforce that will be producing the product. The next account illustrates an aspect of this problem.

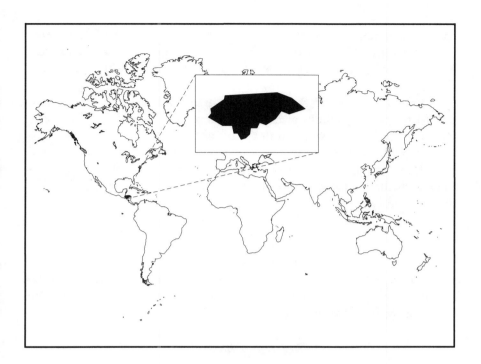

# BUILDING BLOCKS

One large international electronics manufacturer started a plant in a Central American country, taking advantage of the low cost of labor available in that market. Millions of dollars were spent constructing a building with excellent lighting and ventilation, new machinery, and state-of-the-art computers with the latest software. Ads announcing the available positions were placed in the local newspapers and this, along with the word of mouth of friends of friends, attracted hundreds of applicants. About 250 direct labor and 75 indirect labor employees were subsequently hired.

A dozen of these employees were hired as supervisors to train and oversee the newly hired operators. The quality specifications for the individual plant operations were provided (in English) by the parent company. Since the training occurred while the machinery the operators would use was still arriving, the training tended to be a bit theoretical;

hands-on experience would await the installation of the equipment. Quality control norms had been set by the parent company and were based on the production standards of experienced workers in the United States.

Initial estimates by the parent company indicated that the plant should reach profitability after twelve months of operation. Two years after its inception, it was still not profitable.

A step-by-step analysis performed by company auditors indicated that the major problem was poor quality control. An outside management consulting firm was contracted to train the supervisors and instructors in quality control.

## Analysis
### What happened?

Plant profitability was adversely affected by defective product. Recognizing this, the company contracted a management consultant firm to train those responsible for quality control.

### What really happened?

When the management consulting firm tested the supervisors and instructors in the basic skills needed to exercise effective quality control, it became apparent that they could not perform basic arithmetic operations nor measure properly with micrometers or even rulers. This hindered their ability to adhere to the quality specifications. Certain dimensions of the parts would be mistakingly rejected or accepted depending upon the misuse of the measuring devices. Quality was subjectively judged by operators and supervisors who thought they were applying objective standards. Even though the quality standards were going to be difficult to meet (because they were based on the output of experienced U.S. workers), without workers with certain critical skills such as calibration, the standards were never going to be met without more training than the workers received. (It is not a realistic option to lower the quality standards.)

While the Central American workforce at large contains many individuals with the necessary skills for the job, hiring procedures did not screen for these skills. In fact, the criteria listed in the ads mentioned things such as "hard working" and "secondary school graduate" (for clerical positions it identified "attractive appearance" and "secondary school diploma'' as criteria); specific skills, such as calibrating parts, were not mentioned. At the time of the hiring, the local people in charge of the plant start-up did not themselves know exactly which skills were relevant.

### *What can the management consulting firm do now?*

Testing and training are critical to organizing a successful work team. You need to have employees with the necessary capacity to perform their jobs effectively. As one witty production manager said, "*Si no me das el arroz, ¿cómo puedo cocinar?,*" which translates into English as "If you don't give me rice, how can I cook?" When you do not screen for the skills you need, you shouldn't be too surprised when your hires lack critical skills. Since it is not practical to fire large numbers of the workforce, the option is to develop the needed skills through on-the-job training. And that is just what the consulting firm did—it based a crash training program on the critical deficiencies that became evident during testing.

However, there were other personnel deficiencies.

The engineers spent most of their time in their offices and did not mix with the blue-collar workers. Accountability was ephemeral. The outside consultant told them somewhat facetiously that they would be using their offices solely as storage facilities. They had to spend their time on the floor with the workers. Each engineer was put in charge of a specific work team and held accountable for the team's production (after defects were taken into account).

Disciplinary procedures for absenteeism and tardiness and quality existed, but they were not being followed. Existing procedures for testing the quality of product, for returning defective work, for completing weekly training curves were not followed. Discussions with the plant foreman and the union steward put these procedures back in place.

### *How can this situation be avoided in the future?*

High-level company managers tended to see expansion in terms of materialistic things (lighting, ventilation, cafeteria, square feet), but the investment in training the workers in their job functions was low. In many highly industrialized countries, the labor force in some industries tends to be highly skilled, with supervisors and operators who have years of experience in industry (Joe's father and grandfather also worked in a steel mill). There will be a certain realm of knowledge such as basic arithmetic and literacy which you will assume each worker possesses. Where these conditions are lacking in the workforce, on-the-job training must be provided by the company. For the trainers to be effective, you need to know the educational and work background of the people you are training. If you do not test them or question them, you run the risk of gearing the training at too basic or too advanced a level.

When working in developing countries, the level and type of training needed by supervisors and operators change. You don't have a workforce that has decades of experience in the industry. Consequently, there must be a *much greater* investment in training the workers than might be needed for the workforce in industrial nations.

---

# Know the Workforce

Many, sometimes most, industrial workers in developing nations come from a history of work in agriculture. Success in agriculture revolves around the seasonal harvests, whereas in industrialized plants it depends on the successful execution of a number of daily activities with the objective of reaching daily production goals. In a successful agricultural work environment there often exists a command/execute relationship between the boss and the workers. The workers are dependent on the *patrón* for most decision-making. It is no wonder that when they enter into an industrialized work environment without the requisite training, they struggle. They are not accustomed to making decisions every five minutes. But the success of industrialized operations depends on this skill. The agrarian background of much of the modern workforce in developing nations may be part of the reason why their supervisors often focus on single tasks. Quite often the supervisor is concentrating on tossing one ball in his hand, and, when you ask him to juggle two balls, he drops the first ball. When additional tasks are required of these workers, prior tasks often are abandoned or neglected. An effective supervisor needs to be able to juggle several balls at the same time.

You must plan ahead for this and ensure that follow-up is done to verify the continued execution of all tasks and responsibilities. A good rule to follow is to assume that *any* procedure or system will not be implemented successfully unless *active* follow-up is done to ensure that those responsible play their part in making it work.

At this Central American manufacturing plant, the supervisors and management did not have the (human) tools to achieve high levels of productivity. Testing the employees (preferably before they were hired) could have identified the knowledge base of the plant's supervisors. In this case, there was an abundance of candidates in the market who could perform basic mathematics and work a ruler, but they could not be identified without testing.

There were supervisors and in-line samplers who were not capable of properly interpreting the quality specifications that are an integral part of any manufacturing plant. Without them, quality becomes subjective rather than objective, leading to different interpretations of what is acceptable quality. Use of inconsistent criteria often leads to quality problems, and these lead in turn to increased production costs.

# Paralysis

While planning can lead to efficient project implementation, it can become an end in itself, preventing everyone from implementing anything because they are stuck in an interminable planning phase.

After market conditions have been investigated, the workforce assessed in terms of its production capability, and other components of effective planning accomplished, there remain two more big impediments to production. The next account identifies one of them: a consultant wrestles with the problem of making a training program practical.

## LET'S JUST PLAN TO DO IT

The overall training goal was to assist teachers in implementing an innovative interdisciplinary curriculum based on resolving local community problems. Students would learn math, natural science, and language skills in the process of cultivating a school garden (which would produce food for the snack period) or by assisting in designing and measuring the parameters of latrine construction for the school, for example.

The specifics of the first envisioned training session for the rural teachers, a two-day affair, were contained on two pages of topic headings.

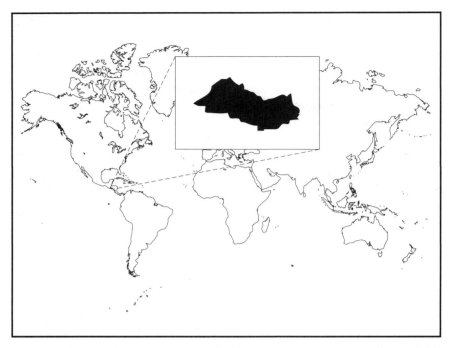

The plan was to provide lectures on the topics to be covered, topics such as lesson planning, curriculum development, and testing. The team was stuck on abstract concepts.

Walter, the outside consultant, asked the team to brief him on why each topic had been included. Thanking the team for its orientation, Walter suggested they meet again the next day to further explore how each topic could best be presented at the training session.

For two hours daily over the next three weeks, Walter led the team in active give-and-take sessions on how to make the training much more practical, on how the topics they wanted covered could be made to speak directly to the needs of each teacher-participant. One idea, for instance, was to provide a brief five- or ten-minute theoretical overview to a large group of rural teachers, followed by each trainee participating in a small group of peers who taught the same grade levels in the same type of school (one-room school, children who spoke the same regional language). These small groups would produce learning units for their students, units they could use in the following week of classes. Each learning unit would translate each agenda topic into practical learning activities for their rural students.

This was tough going and two hours a day of highly focused discussions on how to make a given agenda item more practical, with the consultant alternating between playing the role of devil's advocate and head cheerleader, was about all the team (or Walter) could take. After Walter left for the day, the team would redraft a portion of the training agenda and elaborate on the next agenda topic.

Eventually, the team did produce a reasonably practical workshop design that appealed to the teachers' need to do something in the next class following the workshop.

## Analysis

### *What happened?*

The training curriculum was stuck on abstract concepts.

### *What really happened?*

The fruits of the innovative curriculum were not reaped. The trainers' focus on abstract concepts and lecturing impeded the harvest of practical rewards.

### *What can Walter do now?*

Walter did the right thing. He got the teachers to look more at the needs of the community and devise practical applications to meet those needs.

### *How can this situation be avoided in the future?*

Keep the desired outcomes in sight, and tailor the approach to produce the desired results, but anticipate that you will have to provide a rationale for this approach. Further, you will need to provide an example—a model or template—for the clients to see what a practical approach looks like.

---

The other impediment to production is the extreme. In the next example, a consultant cures an almost terminal case of analysis paralysis.

# HOW MANY TEACHERS DID YOU SAY YOU TRAINED?

Poirot, an educational consultant from Belgium, was invited by an international donor agency to help the Ministry of Education in Zaire,

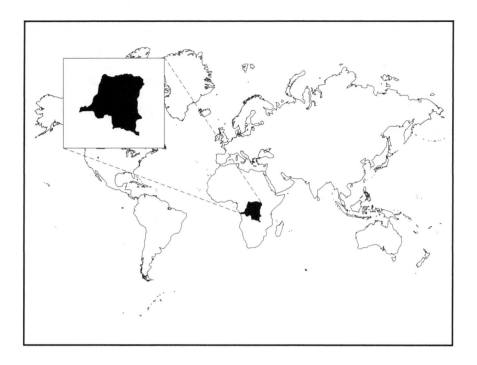

a large country in central Africa and a former Belgian colony, to prepare for a large-scale training project for rural teachers. The four-year, nine-million-dollar project aimed at increasing the efficiency of rural education, a system in which few children reached the second grade of primary school. Only four percent of the children who began first grade completed sixth grade. The envisioned training was meant to improve the quality of instruction and, as a consequence, transform these dismal statistics.

The Ministry of Education created a small task force and housed it in a large but relatively autonomous unit of the Ministry where, it was thought, the project would be reasonably protected from the stifling red tape that engulfed much of the rest of the Ministry.

By the end of the third year of the project, however, only five percent of the budget had been spent and *no* teachers had been trained.

At this point the donor agency contracted Poirot, a troubleshooter who was well versed in the country's educational needs and practices, to find out what the problem was, and, if possible, to break the logjam. He was told to be tactful, but that he was free to describe his role to the Ministry in any way he wished and to proceed in any fashion that might yield results without straining relations between the donor agency and the Ministry.

Poirot presented himself before the unit's deputy director, a woman he had known for some years. (The director dealt with political liaison, while the deputy director was in charge of the day-to-day operations of the unit.) While a secretary served tea, the deputy director provided Poirot with an overview of the teacher training project. Poirot found the overview almost incomprehensible. He couldn't make sense out of what she was saying. A few questions aimed at clarifying the situation only elicited further obfuscations. At the conclusion of the baffling and be-fogged overview, Poirot thanked the deputy director for the "helpful" orientation and for her support of his efforts to "lend a few weeks of technical assistance" to the task force. The deputy director then assigned a room for the task force to work with the consultant and called the task force together. She introduced Poirot to the group, some six professionals, and left him to his devices.

Poirot explained that he was available to help if they felt he could do them any good, and invited them to give him an overview of the project, which they did. Poirot asked lots of questions, many of them pointed but good-humored. It seems they had been busy for three years planning for the teacher training sessions, but they didn't actually have a detailed agenda for the first training session, let alone a date for its occurrence. The task force and the consultant engaged in several hours of good-natured but wary testing of each other. "Let's begin working tomorrow on a specific agenda for the first training session," Poirot suggested. The task force members displayed an uneasy sense that their routine was going to be disturbed in ways they didn't especially welcome.

Poirot had two aces up his sleeve. One was the clout that came as a result of being hired by the funding agency. This translated into perceived power. The second advantage was the result of Poirot's having worked for many years as a consultant with various units of the Ministry in Kin-shasa—he was known and respected. Although he didn't know any of the members of the task force, he knew that they would ask around and that the feedback probably would be positive.

The next morning Poirot arrived at the meeting and received a friendly greeting. The members of the task force were smiling, like ca-nary-fed cats.

"After you left yesterday we discussed the situation and decided that you didn't really understand the project very well," the group's leader said. "So we gathered together all of the documentation on the project. We suggest that you read it and then we can talk again."

On the very large conference table, carefully stacked, were papers that formed a $7' \times 3' \times 2'$ mountain. Maybe six months' reading if you're a speed reader. Planning documents and memos comprised the major share.

This consulting project had reached a critical moment.

## INTERIM ANALYSIS

Two issues were before the troubleshooter. One was major: the group had not been able to get out of its planning mode. Why? But it was the second issue that was going to determine whether Poirot's leadership would be accepted by the group. They had checked his efforts by, in effect, telling him to take the project written documents and go away and get lost.

There were several options open to Poirot.

He could good-naturedly agree to study the gathered documents for a few days or a week or so, then reconvene the group. This would demonstrate his flexibility and would, perhaps, yield the key to understanding why the group had spent three years in planning a four-year project—with no signs that the planning period was over. There were two disadvantages to this approach. First, it would break the momentum toward group action (if only for a few days). Second, it would relinquish Poirot's leadership role in the group before it had been convinced of the need to stop planning and start training teachers. Poirot's role as a change agent would be left to the vagaries of future negotiation with the group. Still, this option seemed reasonable and relatively safe.

Another option open to Poirot was to pit his will against that of the group and insist on forging ahead to the implementation stage of the project without having properly grounded himself in the project's antecedents. This option seemed to carry more risks than the first option. First, if he alienated the group, he was assured of failure, and a refusal to read the material would be a direct challenge to the group. Second, there is a reasonable presumption that he could have learned valuable information by reading the documentation (even though there was a huge amount of it!). Poirot's authority rested on the group's shaky assumption that he had the blessing of the unit's director (or at least the deputy director) and that the donor agency had probably given him whatever authority was needed. (In reality he did not have this authority.) Still, even if by bluff his (implied) authority were recognized by the group, they could easily sabotage his efforts if they wanted to. On the other hand, it would be optimal if he could establish a lofty place for himself in the group's pecking order while maintaining the group's morale and willingness to work toward the project's training stage—and do this without a break in momentum.

## POIROT'S SPLIT-SECOND DECISION

This is what Poirot did. (He had maybe five seconds to decide which approach to use.)

Poirot turned, looked at the mountains of paperwork, and laughed. Turning back to the group he complimented them (with a big smile on his face) on the thoroughness of their planning and then said (still smiling) that he didn't have any intention of reading a single one of the documents. He was not there to help them do what they obviously did so well—planning. Rather he was there to help them implement their planning. The fact remained, he told them, that after all that planning not a single teacher had yet been trained. "Why is that?" he asked them.

What emerged was that each time the group would plan a step, they would submit their plans to higher authority for approval. The group would then, while awaiting the approvals that never came, plan the next step. After three years they had lots of planning documents and accompanying memos requesting permission to implement the plans, but no green light to implement them.

"That must really frustrate you," Poirot said.

The group's response was unanimous: it certainly did.

"Well," Poirot bluffed, "that's going to change now. What we need to do is make the detailed agenda for the first training session. It will get approved." Poirot intimated that he had special knowledge that conditions were going to change.

After three years of fruitless planning, the group was delighted with the prospect of getting the show on the road. They vested considerable faith in the magical intervention of the street-wise consultant. Meanwhile, Poirot set about making his prophecy (things were going to change) self-fulfilling. He needed to orchestrate some critical feedback from the donor agency to the Minister of Education and to the unit's head.

Two months later, 850 teachers were trained in four different locations.

## Analysis
### *What happened?*
The project staff appeared to be incompetent. After three years of planning, only five percent of the budget had been expended and not a single teacher had been trained.

### *What really happened?*
Higher-level administrators had not maintained the level of priority after the previous Minister—the one who had wanted the project—had been replaced, and the administrators were skittish about expending the funds to get the project going. (The administrators were, after all, personally responsible for the expended funds; it was better to have a project that did not perform well than to misappropriate funds.)

### *What can Poirot do now?*
He explained the situation to the funding agency, and they raised the priority of the project through talks with the Minister of Education. The Minister, in turn, put the director of the unit under pressure to perform. About the time the backstage politicking began to show results, the curriculum task force had planned for specific training to occur. Their plans were promptly approved.

### *How can this misunderstanding be avoided in the future?*
In many cases, contract clauses have a mechanism for cutting off project funds if certain benchmarks have not been achieved. But in this case,

the problem was that the project was not spending enough money. Suspension of the project wouldn't have saved much money (that was the problem, they weren't spending much), nor would it have provided an incentive for the Ministry to salvage a project about which the current leaders felt lukewarm.

The key to project implementation was twofold: to keep the issue alive through high-level policy dialogues with Ministry officials, especially after a change in personnel at the top; and to monitor task force accomplishments and bottlenecks on a regular basis.

Young professionals, especially, have more practice planning projects than implementing them. The third world is full of very accomplished planners. Indeed, in labor-intensive countries there is some virtue in employing many people in make-work jobs, but when the planned project holds the promise of increasing economic opportunity, it is worth thinking about implementing it.

Avoid analysis paralysis. It's like a child's penchant for "thinking about" cleaning the bedroom without actually doing it.

---

### ⌈ TOOLBOX ⌉
# Planning

- Do at least as much advance research and planning for your overseas project as you would do back home.

- Assume that your market is made up of a number of segments, each with differing tastes. Assume also that diverse cultural segments are an important part of this stratification.

- Do a market survey to make sure you haven't lost touch with the consumer. One way to do this is through stratified, randomly selected focus groups.

- Assess the skills of your overseas workers so you can estimate production levels.

- Plan a training program to fit the project's and the workers' needs.

## TOOLBOX
# Implementation

- At the first signs of analysis paralysis, check the decision-making style of the organization. If it is rigidly top-down, break the logjam by going to the top, perhaps through indirect pressure. If it is a more egalitarian organization, find the incentives for increased effort and apply them to the right people.

- One reason implementation is postponed is that necessary personnel have not been hired. Why? Circumstances beyond human control? Part-time manager?

- Another reason for analysis paralysis is that the prerequisite for implementation (for example, rental of facilities, purchase of equipment, arrival of supplies) has been delayed. Why? Pressure and/or incentives need to be applied at the right points.

# 10

# Sponsorship and Ownership

## *What Happens After You Leave?*

After planning for implementation, your task as manager or consultant is to assist in the effective implementation of the project, including what it takes to build the local ownership that will set the stage for long-lasting results. This involves training local people to implement the contract specifications and to sustain the gains after the outside managers and consultants have left.

## Leaving Your Project in Good Hands

After you get a contract, your costs hinge on how efficiently you move from planning to implementation to long-term ownership of the project purposes. Delays can sour the sweetness of the deal.

To sustain the results you have worked for, you have to help the hosts "buy into" the project; they have to feel that it is *their* project. To do this, you have to train local people to implement the project. (You also need to involve them in the planning.)

This is easier said than done.

It is often counterproductive to use the training styles with which the local people feel most comfortable. This is true, for instance, when the local style is to lecture on theoretical issues (and then to test recall) when the desired outcome of the training is to prepare local supervisors or workers to achieve more efficiency though specific changes in their

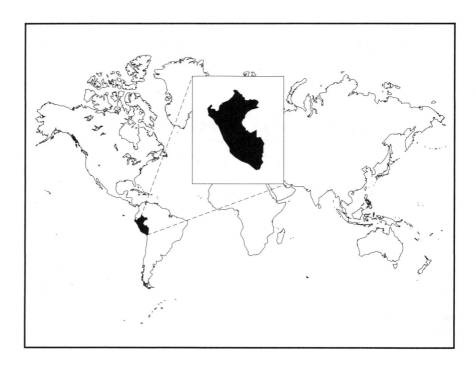

work habits and through creative problem-solving. We saw this in the preceding chapter's account of Walter in El Salvador. In the next example, the problem posed by traditional learning styles is etched in relief.

# A VISITING PROFESSOR'S SEMESTER ABROAD

Maurice, an anthropology professor from Kansas, was delighted to hear that he'd been accepted as a visiting professor for a semester in the Catholic University in Lima, Peru. Maurice had all the skills he needed for the task: he was fluent in Spanish, had previous experience in Peru, had five years' successful experience teaching the course they wanted him to teach (physical anthropology), and was motivated.

From the beginning, the evening class of eighty-five students, mostly teachers themselves, was rowdy. This was especially true when Maurice asked them questions. They were quietest when copying things from the chalkboard. One day after discussing dominant and recessive genes, during a class period aimed at a discussion of the probability (or improbability) of a genetic link to criminal behavior, Maurice discussed two classic sociological studies of this issue (the 1875 study of the Jukes and the 1912 study of the Kallikaks). In one, five generations previously, a good Quaker lad had a liaison with a retarded servant, and a child was born. Repenting his reprobative ways, he married a good Quaker maiden and raised a family. Tracing the descendants of the Quaker lad—the illegitimate and the legitimate—across five generations produced a startling finding. The offspring of the lad with the Quaker maiden were doctors, lawyers, and such, while the children born of the unfortunate liaison with the retarded servant were thieves, paupers, liars, drunkards, and such. Thus, it was concluded by the investigators, there was a clear genetic link to criminality. The retarded servant had passed on the gene to her illegitimate child, and he in turn had passed it on to his descendants for another four generations.

To provide more of the details of this famous case, Maurice used the whole chalkboard in diagraming the family tree of both branches for five generations. The students appeared quite content while they copied everything on the board, including annotations such as "suspected of being a horse thief."

When they were done, Maurice asked the students why this study is fatally flawed. Pandemonium hit the class. The students could not believe they had heard correctly. The student body president, a clean-cut young man in suit and tie, stood beside his desk and asked, incredulously:

"Sir, do you mean that for the last half hour we have been learning a theory that is not correct?"

"That is correct," replied Maurice. "Now where do you see the flaws?"

"You mean we have been wasting our time learning something that is false," continued the student.

"No, you have not been wasting your time, and yes, it is false. Now why do you think it is false?"

"You tell us, you're the professor," replied the student somewhat sarcastically.

Maurice wanted them to note the hearsay character of many of the descriptions of the seamy side of the family, the environmental differences which provided very different opportunities to each branch of the lad's offspring, the complete absence of criminal behavior on the "good" side of the family, and the almost total absence of "good" behavior on the other side. The zinger, of course, is that in none of the hereditary patterns of genes would it be possible for the "defective" gene to have been inherited in the reported pattern. Even if the offending gene were a simple dominant gene, the likelihood of the children inheriting it from a carrier parent would be only 50 percent.

The more Maurice tried to get the students to examine the data, the more the class rebelled.

Facing each class became a torture. Maurice began to experience physical difficulties before each class. He would break out in a cold sweat, have diarrhea, and his head began to ache. The students became increasingly uncontrollable. Mutiny was in the air; students began complaining to other faculty members and to the dean. Maurice couldn't believe he was failing; he had a reputation for being an excellent teacher.

## Analysis
### What happened?

The students were undisciplined and disrespectful of the American teacher.

### What really happened?

The confidence of the students was eroding fast. They had been successful under a traditional methodology—one that Maurice did not use. Their concern for doing well in the class quickly turned to anxiety. One way to solve their problem was to get rid of the offending teacher, Maurice.

### What could Maurice have done?

Desperate, Maurice sought out a colleague whom he knew to have taught a course a year or two before at the same university. Although Maurice anticipated difficulty in communicating his plight, his colleague immediately recognized the class behavior.

"The same thing happened to me when I taught introductory psychology," the colleague admitted.

"Good," said Maurice. "What did you do to overcome the problems?"

"I quit," replied the colleague.

Maurice, no quitter, returned to the classroom. Knowing the students enjoyed copying things from the board, he drew a Mendelian example of simple dominant (A,B) and recessive (a,b) traits. He drew a tall skinny squash (AA + aa) and a short fat squash (BB + bb) at the top of the board. Underneath, he listed the 32 genetic combinations that this hybridization might produce (Aa + Bb, AA + BB, Aa + Ba . . .) The students were happy again.

Maurice then asked the class which of all the combinations was the most interesting. Instantly, the group became "The Class from Hell." At this rate, it wouldn't be long before he was called to the dean's office to hear some unpleasant news.

He had to do something else.

Maurice thought of an old veteran professor from the National University, a decidedly more difficult student environment than the more elite Catholic University, and made an appointment to see him. Again, Maurice had no difficulty communicating the situation.

"Ah," said the veteran teacher, Licenciado Estrada. "A clash in learning methodologies! You are using an inquiry approach, and they are expecting a traditional lecture mode."

"But what can I do?" asked a still desperate Maurice.

Estrada said, "Do these four things:

"First, explain to the class why you are all having these difficulties. Explain that there is a difference in teaching techniques. Describe the methodology they are used to (teacher lectures, students copy, teacher tests, students regurgitate).

"Second, tell them what you are trying to do: to get them to discover patterns; to think for themselves.

"Third, tell them why your method is better: as the 'facts' change, they have a method of . . .

"And last, tell them that in the final analysis, the students must decide for themselves: the future of their education—and the future of Peru—is in their hands."

Maurice returned to the class and used the whole period to cover the four points. When he finished, the class was silent. Pushing his luck, Maurice asked if there were any questions or comments. A scruffy, surly-looking student in the back row, left-hand corner, raised his hand. Maurice pretended not to see it; he repeated his intemperate question. No other hands were raised. In resignation, Maurice called on the student who, like a Middle East terrorist, always managed to maintain a three-day growth of beard on his frowning face.

"I like what you said about the future of our education is in our hands." Maurice waited for the worst. "Thank you."

The class applauded.

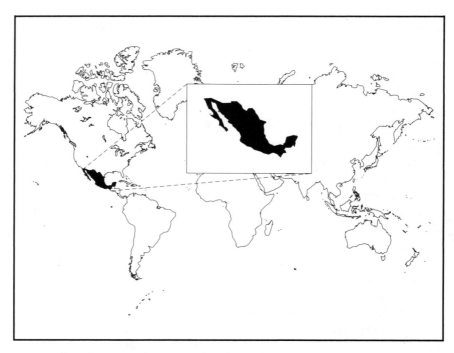

During the next class, Maurice drew the two pumpkins on the board and filled in all 32 cells, stepped back, and asked, "Which cell is the most interesting?"

Eighty-five heads inclined forward in intense concentration. After a while, a student raised her hand and identified the cell. "Right. And why is this the most interesting?" Maurice probed. Another student raised his hand. "Because its combination of genetic traits is different from its parents in a way that none of the other cells is." And the class was off and running.

### How can this problem be avoided in the future?

The next time this situation occurred (during an exchange lectureship in a Central American university), Maurice used some hindsight and very early in the course explained—with examples—the points suggested by the veteran teacher. It worked like a charm.

---

The next example illustrates what can happen when you forget that Murphy's Law is universal.

# PUTTING YOUR PLANS IN COLD STORAGE

In Mexico City a large consortium was constructing two manufacturing plants to build refrigerators—one to make the plastic parts for the refrigerators and the other to perform various tooling operations and to assemble the final product. The management consultant's role was to train fifteen engineers in an analytical operator training methodology.

The fifteen engineers would then train supervisors on the machinery using these techniques. The supervisors would, in turn, train the operators. This organization's goal was to develop two state-of-the-art plants complete with a JIT (Just-in-Time), TQC (Total Quality Control), TEI (Total Employee Involvement) system. (You gotta love those catchy acronyms.) The objective was to have one operator run several machines. This was possible because of the cycle times of the different machines. A workforce skilled in operating several machines would reduce the cost of direct labor, and this would create a competitive advantage in the marketplace.

This particular training methodology was developed in the United States during World War II to promote higher productivity in industrialized plants that supported the wartime effort by reducing the time necessary to train operators to make war arms. The methodology is based on breaking an operation down into the separate motions that a skilled operator does to perform a given operation. Exercises are developed to train operators to perform the separate segments of the operation as well as a skilled operator. There are four types of exercises: the basic exercises to develop the basic dexterity and knowledge that an operator will need to be effective; the parts exercises to develop the efficiency that a skilled operator has in performing a certain part of the operation; the single-cycle exercises that require performing a complete cycle of the operation at 100 percent efficiency; and the stamina build-up exercises to develop the ability to perform at 100 percent efficiency for progressively longer periods of time, until the operator can work at 100 percent for a whole day. These exercises have quality and time-efficiency goals consistent with what is expected of a fully trained operator working at an incentive pace.

When it came time to use the developed exercises, the project ran into trouble. The machinery did not arrive as scheduled. The Mexican management assured the consultant that it would soon arrive.

The delays in procuring the machinery continued, leading to other problems. The client requested a build-up schedule in order to know when to hire the operators. The hiring schedule was contingent on the equipment arrival. Due to the delays, this schedule, however, had to be revised each time an updated equipment arrival schedule was made. Dozens of operators were hired based on the ever-changing build-up schedule. They would spend their days sweeping the floors because the machinery had not arrived. Cross-training the operators in machine operation and sweeping floors did not appear the best way to go, however. Some excellent workers got bored and found employment with other firms.

# Analysis
### What happened?
The less-than-hands-on training continued with the engineers in the hope that the equipment would soon arrive. Meanwhile, new machine operators were steadily being hired.

### What really happened?
The engineers had reached the point in their training where they needed to work with the actual machines, but the machines did not arrive. Time was wasted updating build-up schedules when the equipment arrival schedules constantly changed.

### What can the consultant do now?
Nothing. The fat lady sang.

What could have been done differently? Postpone the engineer training and hiring until the equipment arrived.

### How can this situation be avoided in the future?
The purpose of planning is to ensure that the objectives of any given undertaking are achieved in the most efficient and effective way. Sometimes, as the last chapter pointed out, we become so engrossed in planning that we forget that we cannot accomplish the planning objective until the planning process stops and the implementation begins. Planning is not an end in itself, but the means to reach the end. Still, training

in the abstract, rather than hands-on training, is more the rule than the exception. It's like telling a child how he needs to swing the baseball bat, but never tossing him the ball to hit. The child becomes frustrated.

It was clear that the build-up plan continuously changed as the machine delays continued. Recognizing that the equipment delays would continue, they could have chosen not to hire anyone until the machines were on-site. This would have eliminated (a) the cost of paying dozens of operators' salaries and benefits for several months, until the equipment arrived; (b) the time invested by a manager in managing these operators; and (c) the low morale of operators, who were hired to run expensive machinery, rather than more modestly priced brooms. And, of course, it would have shortened the time needed to train the engineers by making the training practical rather than abstract.

---

While education and training in many highly industrialized countries tends to stress practical applications, in many other countries, Mexico included, more emphasis typically is placed on theoretical issues. This leads to commonplace conundrums. Projects are started with an understanding by senior management of the desired objectives, but little thought is given to problems that will arise in the actual implementation. The following case is an excellent example.

# HOW TO CULTIVATE THE WORK ETHIC SO IT WORKS FOR YOU

In one leather goods plant in New Jersey, a state on the northeastern coast of the United States, a management consulting firm was contracted to set up modules in a seasonal build-up to meet the high demand. The objective was to make the new operators productive as soon as possible. Charlie Moore was sent to set up the screening procedures and to train the selected workers.

The workforce at this U.S. plant was a cross-section of Latin America. There were operators from Mexico to Argentina. There were also operators from other countries, including several from the former Soviet Union. The production manager was Colombian. He acted as a liaison between the non-Spanish-speaking Jewish management and the workers.

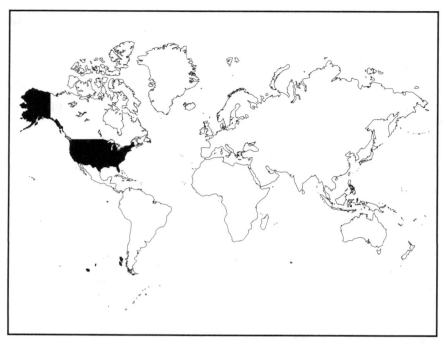

To hire the best candidates from the labor pool, dexterity tests and a stability interview were administered. Having passed the selection process, they were put through a one-day orientation and a two-day analytical training program to develop basic skills necessary in the leather goods trade. As part of the training, good work habits were developed and the trainees were encouraged to reach 100 percent efficiency levels.

One hundred fifty mostly minority people who successfully underwent the basic training were hired for the seasonal upturn and were set up in modules, ranging in size from nine to thirteen people. About half the trainees were interspersed throughout experienced modules. Since there were no vacant slots in many of the modules, and it was not convenient to break up some of the experienced modules, the other half of the trainees were assigned to new modules that were guided by a "module leader" who had a thorough understanding of how to put together the leather product with high quality standards.

The results were astounding. Within three to four weeks the new modules were outperforming the experienced modules staffed mostly by people who had not gone through the new selection and training process.

## Analysis

### *What happened?*

Happy story: the selection and training program worked.

### *What really happened?*

Unhappy story: the new trainees who joined experienced modules did not contribute to increased productivity. Why? When this was examined more closely, it was discovered that the trainees who went into the experienced modules rose— or fell—to the level of that module. If the module was at 60 percent efficiency, then the trainee would plateau at about 60 percent. In the experienced modules the trainees often were negatively influenced by experienced operators with poor work habits. They made frequent trips to the washroom and spent excessive time socializing with others.

### *What can the company do now?*

It can train all of the workers in good work habits.

### *How can this situation be avoided in the future?*

Sometimes managers are reluctant to invest in training programs because they hold negative stereotypes of the workers, especially if the workforce is made up predominantly of minority people. But certain fundamentals remain true across races and cultures. In this plant the success of the worker was affected to a great extent by how management was able *to manage the expectations* of the new workers. This explains how trainees were able to achieve such high levels of productivity in such a short period.

---

## Successful Training

- Make your training outcome-oriented.

- Schedule the training to be contingent upon the at-hand availability of necessary materials and equipment to ensure that the training is hands-on practical.

- "Sell" your hands-on training approach by explaining the differences between your approach and the more traditional approaches the client may be used to, explain why your approach is better for the task at hand, and invite the client's cooperation.

- Show confidence in the people who will be taking over after you leave. Not only will this help them do an excellent job, but also it will bolster their "political" position within the organization, and this, too, will give them a better shot at success.

- Bring your counterparts into the decision-making process so they have a stake in the outcome.

- Identify a number of people (not just one) who will be project sponsors after you leave.

- Stay in touch after you leave the project.

# 11

# Overcoming Culture Clash

The key to getting the most out of an overseas assignment is to participate in the host country's institutional life. How do you do this? Is there a local government agency where you can sign up for membership? With all the demands adapting to the new work environment, how do you get R & R? This chapter provides pointers on how to enjoy your intercultural sojourn.

## Immersion in the Host Culture

Working in a multicultural setting can put some gray hairs on your head. At home you knew how to get results and were in control. Abroad, company procedures, politics, and job functions often baffle you. It is not uncommon to feel you left "control" at the airport. Your old routines and support network of friends, family, and the familiar now lie thousands of miles away in a different world. As a stranger in a strange land you will have to develop a new routine and social life from scratch. This section suggests ways to overcome the grunts and groans associated with intercultural contact—the culture clash that was described in chapter 1, "Coping with Culture Clash."

In this final chapter you will learn to temper your expectations of what you may be able to accomplish early on. The Big Key to opening the door to mental health and happiness is to participate in the host country's institutional life. This participation sets the stage for having a lot of fun.

For as far as the eye can see, multicultural forces are everywhere: in the media, at work, in the community, and even in the home. The best way to adjust to this diversity is by interacting with people from other cultural backgrounds, followed by some self-reflection when things misfire, when there is a strong likelihood that miscommunication has reared its embarrassing head. In a multicultural world, ignorance—not familiarity—breeds contempt. The more you interact the more you will learn to understand how other people react under varying circumstances.

# Work Space

The great challenge in moving abroad is the number of adjustments you must make at one time. Many things you take for granted, such as the availability of frozen dinners in the supermarket, prove frustrating. You must learn to adapt to a new job, community, country, and culture. Each one of these adjustments requires you to delve into an enigmatic world of interrelated actions.

What is involved in adjusting to a new job? Early on you will need to meet the people with whom you will work and learn their job functions. Whom do you see to get a given task done? New procedures and new ways of achieving results may have to be learned. There may be many communication problems resulting from language barriers. For example, it is highly probable that you felt a high level of competence and comfort in the job you left. When you arrive at a foreign locale, this sense is often lost, which can lead to a sense of inadequacy. Most of this book has dealt with various approaches to dealing with these workplace issues.

But there are two other settings you will be dealing with, the community and the residence.

# Community Space

Adjustments to a new country and community include learning the transportation, telephone, and mail systems. One of the first things you must learn in a foreign country is where and how to get your clothes washed. Nobody wants to be around a stinker.

For the sojourner it is not any one particular adjustment that is so demanding; rather, it is the sum of all the adjustments. Although the adjustments are greater as you enter a country far different from your own (from the United States to Kenya vs. from the United States to Canada, for example), it is sometimes the more subtle differences in culture that cause the most uneasiness. You expect differences when the contrast between two cultures is dramatic, but the differences in thought and action in relatively similar cultures can put you off as well. It is important to exhibit patience during this ongoing adjustment period.

Much of what you do will take longer than you are accustomed to, from completing your daily ablutions to implementing a training program at work.

Often business people working abroad develop a sense of inadequacy because they find they are not as effective as they were at home. Tempering your expectations will help to alleviate this feeling. First, strive to be functional in the community. Get the lay of the land, discover where the movies, theaters, museums, and sports arenas are. Visit the parks and the stores. Take some local buses. Find out where you can get a copy of *Time* magazine or *U.S. News and World Report.* Ask where people go on their day(s) off. Go there. Be pleasant (remember the U.S. professor and the German baby carriage?). Then gradually raise your expectations. Reward yourself for whatever level of functionality you have achieved on any given day.

It is natural to avoid situations in which you do not feel comfortable. When you move into multicultural space—at home or overseas—it helps to be aware of this tendency. By avoiding contact with people from another culture, you subconsciously build a wall that will leave you feeling isolated (not to mention ignorant of the culture). When you find yourself "a stranger in a strange land" (to borrow the title from Robert Heinlein's wonderful novel), remind yourself that the reason you accepted (or courted) the overseas assignment in the first place was the lure of working somewhere different from home. Intercultural encounters are a challenge, an opportunity to prove your self-reliance, to expand your horizons.

# Home Space

Getting along in your overseas residence is important to your mental health. It may be a hotel, a boardinghouse, a room with a family, or a private apartment. The best study to date of intercultural difficulties within a home setting was done by the sociologist, Raymond L. Gorden. Gorden studied miscommunication that occurred while U.S. college students and Peace Corps volunteers resided in the homes of middle-class hosts in Bogotá, Colombia. Gorden focused on two elements that directly affect how well you fit in: space and role.

The first type of problem (space) occurred because the Americans did not know the proper way to behave in the living room, the bedroom, the bathroom, the kitchen, and so on. For example, the Americans were considered unkempt because they put their shoes in the wrong place in their bedrooms. (They belonged in the closet or the wardrobe.) Others were considered either too forward or too standoffish, depending on when they kept their bedroom door open or closed—and how open or closed they kept it.

The second type of problem that intrigued Gorden concerned inappropriate role relationships the Americans tried to maintain with the various members of the host household. For example, one American male, after "a terrific dinner party" in the host home, attempted to help the señora and the maid afterward by carrying a tray full of dishes into the kitchen. Gorden reports that the sight of a man in the kitchen trying to scrape the dishes was too disturbing to the Colombians' notions of social status and was more distracting than helpful. Another problem faced by middle-class guests was maintaining the proper relationship with domestic help.

There are a few general behaviors we have found useful for "getting into" the host culture, regardless of the culture in which you find yourself.

# A Few Do's

*Look up the friends of friends.* Many societies that seem relatively closed to outsiders open up to friends of friends. Ned, working in Egypt (for the first time) during the annual Ramadan fast, was invited to a Muslim home for the family feast celebrating the end of Ramadan. This was because he was a friend of a friend. Sometimes this will be the only way you will have the chance to see the inside of a home in the country where you are working. By the way, when you are invited into someone's home, accept.

This approach has its disappointments, such as the time in Portugal when one couple went considerably out of their way to visit the friend of a friend in a town outside Lisbon. They conveyed the greetings of the mutual friend, introduced themselves, and were told, *"Muito obrigado; mando muchas lembranças para ela tambem"* ("Thanks. Tell her that I send my regards too"). They were then sent on their way; the whole conversation lasted less than five minutes. In fact, due to the bus schedule, they were stranded overnight. Nevertheless, some of the most memorable travel times have resulted from invitations to stay with the friend-of-a-friend's family for a day or two.

*Enter the institutional life of the society.* A group of philatelists in the United States, interested in collecting the stamps of Guatemala, formed a society. They made contact with the Guatemalan stamp collectors' association and began exchanging newsletters. Over the years, most of the U.S. members of the society made trips to Guatemala to meet the local philatelists. This institutional door has provided the entryway into the greater Guatemalan culture for scores of stamp collectors. There are special-interest clubs of all sorts.

When Ned was younger, he used to make contact with the local judo club (*dojo*) whenever he was going to spend more than a month in the country. Lifelong friendships began this way. Alan prefers to lift weights in local health clubs and to visit museums and art galleries. He, too, began long friendships with people who like to perspire and/or look at pictures.

Churches are another common entry point into a culture. International organizations such as Rotary International offer excellent avenues to meet local people. One of the most egalitarian institutions in Latin America is the volunteer fire station. If you are experienced and are planning to stay for a couple years, join one. There are scores of organizations in most countries that would enjoy your presence.

Classes in almost anything imaginable are offered in urban centers around the globe. Embassies offer language classes. Universities offer semester and often short-term evening classes. Musicians teach music in their living rooms. Artists and potters teach out of a back room or out of doors. These afford opportunities to meet people and learn something to boot. Humans are gregarious animals and need to be around others. If your room does not have a radio, buy one for ten or twenty dollars; we shouldn't be alone too much of the time. (Once in awhile we all do need to get off by ourselves, perhaps with a book.)

*Learn the unpredictable microbehaviors.* There are certain culturally general ways to enhance your entry into most any society, and there are some rituals that can be predicted if you know a few characteristics of the culture. For the most part, though, you have to learn the discrete ways to behave. By way of example, one American educator, Peg Koetsch, in Japan to learn about wood-burning kiln techniques, stopped dinner conversation her first evening with a temple family she was visiting by pouring soy sauce directly onto her rice.

*Help with the chores.* Do the dishes, for example. Well, not if you are a male in a Latin American household. But do help with the daily tasks that people of your gender, age, and status do. Often this calls for judgment. Jacqueline H. Wasilewski, a U.S. consultant studying nonformal education systems in Papua New Guinea, smoothed her entrance into a remote Barai village by staying in a village house when invited—rather than the missionary complex—and by helping the mother of that house do all her daily tasks which included washing the dishes in the stream at the bottom of the ravine. As it turned out, she was the first white, female stranger to have done so. The whole village turned out to watch the dishwashing display. Previously, foreign visitors had stayed in the relative comfort of the "Christian" end of the village or in the missionary compound.

Helping is not a bad strategy when one returns home, either. One well-known Native American, LaDonna Harris (the first woman, by the way, to have run for the vice-presidency of the United States—on Barry Commoner's People's Party ticket in 1980), rolls up her sleeves to help with the chores within a short time of returning to visit Comanche relatives and friends. This shows that she has not been changed by success in the nontribal world; the little girl who didn't speak English until she went to school has not forgotten who she is.

*Read the newspapers, listen to the radio, and watch television* to tune in to what people are talking about. Much human drama is played out on the front page of the local newspaper or on the latest episode of a soap opera. Typically, one of the first habits to be broken during a change in routine caused by travel is keeping up with the news. There often is little choice while traveling; the media are not available. Tune back into what's happening on the local scene even though it may not seem interesting, much less transcendental, at first. It may take a special effort to get back into the topical reading groove, but the results are worth the effort.

Frank was accompanying a young American missionary on an errand in Montevideo, Uruguay. Cutting through an arcade, Frank noticed a little shop that sold records and tapes. He stopped and bought several tapes of folk music. The missionary asked Frank whether he liked "that kind of music." After replying enthusiastically, Frank asked the missionary what kind of Uruguayan music he liked. "Oh," he said, "we are discouraged from listening to the radio. It takes time away from the missionary effort." How sad. It also took time away from developing ties to the culture which might have enhanced the likelihood of establishing rapport with the Uruguayans. The "time is money" attitude diminished the chances that the missionary would reinforce his work by staying in touch with Uruguay and Uruguayans after his tour of duty expired.

*Get to know the country.* Visit the tourist sites. Show an interest in the country. It was remarked in Egypt—the country with the oldest tradition of tourism—that when the new U.S. Secretary of State visited the pyramids of Giza on the outskirts of Cairo, he was the first U.S. Secretary of State to do so. He showed interest in the cultural traditions of the country, and the gesture was appreciated.

*Listen to your mother: eat well and get your sleep.* A well-balanced diet and rest are really important to your ability to function effectively. And on the subject of mothers, write to family and to friends and encourage them to write back; it'll do wonders for your morale. Much of the time abroad is spent waiting for the mail to arrive.

*Talk to other expatriates.* Stranded in the airport in Lagos, Nigeria, on his way to an assignment in India, a researcher struck up a conversation with another traveler who had spent twenty years as an international agricultural consultant. The researcher expressed some trepidation about going to India, a country in which he had never worked before. He was intimidated by the teeming crowds, the diseases, the stark differences in daily life. The eyes of the agricultural consultant lit up. "India," he ruminated. "My favorite country! I spent twelve years there." Just hearing his traveling companion talk about India in such warm terms lowered the researcher's anxiety.

*Show that you are glad to be where you are.* No matter how humble, there's no place like home (or hometown or home country). Show your appreciation for whatever seems appropriate: the air, the sky, the mountains or the plains, the smell of the magnolia. But be honest about it. Well, not brutally honest. You wouldn't say how good it is to be back in Washington, D.C., because of the interesting crime headlines, would you?

*Be interested in the "trivia" of others' lives.* One television talk show host claims that the key to his success is sincere interest in his guests. "When you learn to fake sincerity, you've got it made," he elaborates. At any rate, any "faking" will be limited to the beginning of the relationship. After you get to know the hosts, you will become sincerely interested in the details of their lives. Don't expect everyone to ask about you, by the way. Instead, ask them about how things are going for them. Empathy is consistently associated with intercultural effectiveness.

In some societies, friendliness (generally a good trait) needs to be tempered by social prudence. A blond teenage American was spat upon when he uninhibitedly approached a group of sullen, anti-American men in a Central American marketplace.

*Take personal gifts for the people you will meet*, especially if that is the custom. (Even if it is not the custom, as long as it will not offend or create an unwanted need for them to reciprocate, go ahead and give them a gift such as pens or pins.) One Mexican friend of the authors, Caridad Inda, a nun and Ph.D. linguist who heads a language institute in Guadalajara, buys a lot of small pieces of folk crafts before she visits the United States. She carries them in her pocketbook and gives the little ceramic frogs and other delightful artifacts to friends and acquaintances as she sees them. (On her last trip she gave one author a little brass Lucifer.)

*Learn at least the rudiments of the local language.* William Stewart, the sociolinguist who specializes in dialects of Black English, was asked whether he spoke with the people he studied in standard English or in their local tongue. (At the time, he was studying Gullah, the language of the Brer Rabbit stories.) "From the first day," Stewart replied, "I incorporate the local sounds and turns of phrase as I learn them. People seem to appreciate the effort."

*Learn the local eating etiquette.* Outside the United States, using two hands to eat in Europe and Latin America (usually the knife in the right hand, the fork in the left) will give a better impression than employing the American style of using a fork in the right hand for most eating, including the cutting of soft food, but the difference is not critical. On the other hand, using chopsticks well generates much goodwill in Japan. In many African countries, you eat with your hands. If you eat with your left hand in most Islamic countries, you will achieve instant status as a social outcast. (The left hand is associated with toilet hygiene.)

*Adjust your clothing styles.* When you return to your "native" culture, don't flaunt obviously distinctive ways of dressing unless it is really important to you, perhaps for religious or other cultural reasons. Morgan Rhys returned to Pennsylvania after several years of music study in Italy. He got off the boat wearing a black suit, black hat, and a black cape that would be the envy of Batman. In that instant, Uncle Morgan became family legend; this happened seventy years ago.

One stylish Latin American who lived in her country's capital city used to wash her hair (to remove the fancy hairdo) and put on modest clothing while visiting her family in a rural area of the country so she wouldn't appear like Miss Highhorse visiting her "poor" relatives.

As you try to blend into a society it pays to be alert to pregnant distinctions that carry social meaning. For instance, Ned moved to Italy on a long-term assignment and went to a men's store to buy a beret (*biretto*), the most common hatware of the region. He was partial to black. "No," the clerk told him, "you will like this navy blue one better." Ned insisted on buying a black one while the clerk put considerable effort into trying to sell him a navy blue one. Ned "won" the struggle. When he got back to his apartment, he showed the beret to the Italian neighbors on the other side of the stairwell. They asked if it were a present for a friend. No, Ned told them, it was for himself. "But only priests wear black berets!" exclaimed the astonished neighbors.

It is common for many young Americans who go to Latin America and to other developing nations to "go native" in their dress. They wear sandals, straw hats, and typical indigenous or rural dress. Many Latin Americans wonder why the Americans are dressing as poor peasants (aren't all Americans rich?). On the other side of the coin, urban men in Latin America risk considerable ridicule if they wear brightly colored socks. One hapless gentleman provoked considerable jocularity at a party because he wore light blue socks. None of the women wanted to dance with him.

# A Few Don'ts

*Don't judge life in another culture by your cultural standards.* If you do, you'll miss the unique beauty that each culture has to offer the sympathetic visitor. You wouldn't judge the insides of a digital watch by the insides of an analog watch, would you? Each culture allows its adherents to satisfy universal physical and psychological needs, but each culture provides different ways to accomplish this. Gaining wisdom, to take one example, may be done through silent meditation in one culture, while another prefers the noisy interaction of the marketplace, and still another through capturing—and subsequently shrinking—the head of a worthy adversary.

*Don't speak with more of an accent than you can avoid.* Just because a sound sounds "funny"—or even obscene—to your ears don't avoid using it.

One English-speaking woman living in Mexico thought the o sound of *doctor* (as in Dr. Mata) sounded "ickey." She insisted on using the English sound, as in /dácter/. While she felt more comfortable with this pronunciation, the Mexicans universally thought it sounded unpleasantly weird. Some U.S. visitors purposely avoid rolling their *r*s for the same reason, with the same counterproductive results.

Especially don't speak to your own countrymen in your native language with an acquired accent. A prominent Argentine, of French parents, speaks completely fluent Spanish but with a pronounced French accent. Ned asked a mutual friend about this. "Well," he replied with a cynical smile, "his older brother speaks Spanish without an accent." The implication was that the French accent was an affectation. Conversely, Spanish-speaking students who go to the U.S. for study and return to their homes several years later speaking Spanish with an American accent may be disdained by former friends.

If your surname originated in one of the cultures you are visiting, do pronounce it the ethnically "proper" way. One Chicano from Los Angeles, on a visit to Mexico City, alienated the people he met because he insisted on pronouncing his name, Chavez, in the American way—voicing the 'z' (he should have pronounced it as a voiceless 's' without vibrating his vocal chords) and shifting the stressed syllable from the first to the last (in Spanish the word is written with an accent on the first syllable, *Chávez*).

Many people who learn their mother tongue at home and are not able to use it much outside family settings find themselves at a disadvantage during adolescent or young adult years when they come into contact with strangers who speak the same language. Puerto Rican children raised on the mainland, for example, sometimes distress their Spanish-speaking teachers by addressing them in the familiar *tú* form. Spend a little time to tune up your language skills.

*Don't say much about the country you just left.* Answer casual questions about your home country with brief, upbeat responses. You may add, to reduce envy, that the weather was very hot (or cold), or that the trains were on strike. If the host has a sincere interest in your country, be as brutally honest as you can in your responses: don't echo your government's official view unless you agree with it.

That's about all the advice for now.

We hope that this book's penchant for highlighting cultural missteps experienced by multicultural voyagers in many parts of the world has not unduly increased your anxiety about working in multicultural locales. We have tried to increase awareness of the terrain, not fear of it. Remember Alfred E. Neuman's helpful personal injunction: "What, me worry?" We wish you well on your multicultural assignments. Perhaps we'll run into each other; let's flip to see who pays for a glass of lemonade.

## Having Fun

- Look up friends of friends.

- Enter the institutional life of the country. Go to church. Join a health club. Lift weights. Golf. Jog. Pray.

- Add some skills to your personal repertoire. Learn karate. Take art lessons. Sign up for language classes.

- Read the newspapers. Listen to the radio. Watch TV. Go to plays.

- Get into an after-work routine—particularly on weekends when you may be alone by the telephone.

# References and Further Reading

Abecasis-Phillips, John A. S. *Doing Business with the Japanese*. Lincolnwood, IL: NTC Business Books, 1994.

ALM Consulting, Frere Cholmeley Bischoff, and KPMG Peat Marwick. *Doing Business in Russia*. Lincolnwood, IL: NTC Business Books, 1993.

Adler, Nancy J. *International Dimensions of Organizational Behavior*. Boston: PWS-Kent Publishing, 1986.

Adler, Nancy J., and Dafna N. Izraeli, eds. *Women in Management Worldwide*. Armonk, New York: M. E. Sharpe, 1988.

"American Attitudes Toward Europe: A New Gallup Poll." *Europe*. March 1988, p. 24.

Axtell, Roger E. *Do's and Taboos of Hosting International Visitors*. New York: John Wiley & Sons, 1990.

Axtell, Roger E. *The Do's and Taboos of International Trade: A Small Business Primer*. New York: John Wiley & Sons, 1989.

Bartlett, Christopher A., and Sumantra Ghoshal. *Managing Across Borders: The Transnational Solution*. Cambridge, MA: Harvard Business School Press, 1989.

Binnendijk, Hanns. *National Negotiation Styles*. Washington, DC: U.S. Department of State, Foreign Service Institute, 1987.

Brislin, Richard W., Kenneth Cushner, Craig Cherrie, and Mahealani Yong. *Intercultural Interactions: A Practical Guide*. Newberry Park, CA: Sage, 1986.

Brown, H. Douglas. *Breaking the Language Barrier*. Yarmouth, ME: Intercultural Press, 1991.

Casse, Pierre. *Training for the Multicultural Manager: A Practical and Cross-Cultural Approach to the Management of People.* Washington, DC: SIETAR International, 1982.

Casse, Pierre. *Training for the Cross-Cultural Mind.* Washington, DC: SIETAR International, 1979.

Casse, Pierre, and Surinder Deol. *Managing Intercultural Negotiations: Guidelines for Trainers and Negotiators.* Washington, DC: SIETAR International, 1985.

Copeland, Lennie, and Lewis Griggs. *Going International: How to Make Friends and Deal Effectively in the Global Marketplace.* New York: Random House, 1985.

De Mente, Boye L. *Japanese Etiquette and Ethics in Business*, 6th ed. Lincolnwood, IL: NTC Business Books, 1994.

De Mente, Boye L. *How To Do Business with the Japanese.* Lincolnwood, IL: NTC Business Books, 2nd ed., 1993.

De Mente, Boye L. *Chinese Etiquette & Ethics in Business.* Lincolnwood, IL: NTC Business Books, 1990.

De Mente. Boye L. *Korean Etiquette and Ethics in Business.* Lincolnwood, IL: NTC Business Books, 1988.

Decker, J. S. "Marija Dixon: Building Bridges Between East and West." *Detroit Marketplace.* December 1990, pp. 20-26.

Dowling, Peter J., and Randall S. Schuler. *International Dimensions of Human Resource Management.* Boston: PWS-Kent, 1990.

Edmonson, Munro S. "Neolithic Diffusion Rates." *Current Anthropology* 2 (1961): 71-102.

Engholm, Christopher. *When Business East Meets Business West: The Pacific Rim Guide to Practice and Protocol.* New York: Wiley, 1991.

Farb, Peter. *Word Play: What Happens When People Talk.* New York: Knopf, 1973.

Fieg, John Paul, revised by Elizabeth Mortlock. *A Common Core: Thais and Americans.* Yarmouth, ME: Intercultural Press, 1989. (Includes contrast of Thai and American management styles.)

Gorden, Raymond L. *Interviewing: Strategy, Techniques, and Tactics.* Homewood, IL: Dorsey, 1987.

Gorden, Raymond L. *Living in Latin America: A Case Study in Cross-Cultural Communication.* Lincolnwood, IL: National Textbook Co., 1974.

Grace, George William. *The Linguistic Construction of Reality.* New York: Croom Hellm, 1987.

Graham, John L., and Yoshiro Sano. *Smart Bargaining: Doing Business with the Japanese.* New York: Harper & Row, 1989.

Habert, Kjell, and Arild Lillebo. *Made in Norway: Norwegians as Others See Them.* Bekkestua, Norway: Norwegian School of Management Press, 1988.

Hall, Edward T. *The Silent Language.* New York: Fawcett, 1961.

Hall, Edward T., and Mildred Reed Hall. *Understanding Cultural Differences: Germans, French and Americans.* Yarmouth, ME: Intercultural Press, 1990.

Hall, Edward T., and Mildred Reed Hall. *Hidden Differences: Doing Business with the Japanese.* New York: Anchor Press/Doubleday, 1987.

Harris, Philip R., and Robert T. Moran. *Managing Cultural Differences.* Houston, TX: Gulf Publishing, 3rd ed., 1990.

Hofstede, Geert. *Cultures and Organizations: Software of the Mind.* London and New York: McGraw-Hill, 1991.

Hofstede, Geert. *Culture's Consequences: International Differences in Work-related Values.* Beverly Hills, CA: Sage Publications, 1980.

Hsu, Frances L. K. *Americans and Chinese: Reflections on Two Cultures and Their People.* New York: Holt, Rinehart and Winston, 1970.

Inkeles, Alex, and Daniel J. Levinson. "National Character: The Study of Modal Personality and Sociocultural Systems," in *The Handbook of Social Psychology,* 2nd ed., vol. 4, G. Lindsey and E. Aronson, eds. Reading, MA: Addison-Wesley, 1969.

Kealey, Daniel J. "A Study of Cross-Cultural Effectiveness: Theoretical Issues, Practical Applications." *International Journal of Intercultural Relations* 13, 3 (1989): 387-428.

Kochman, Thomas. *Black and White Styles in Conflict.* Chicago: University of Chicago Press, 1981.

Kohls, L. Robert. *Survival Kit for Overseas Living: For Americans Planning to Live and Work Abroad.* Yarmouth, ME: Intercultural Press, 2nd ed., 1984.

Kraemer, Alfred J. *Development of a Cultural Self-Awareness Approach to Instruction in Intercultural Communication.* Alexandria, VA: Human Resources Research Organization, 1973.

Kras, Eva. *Management in Two Cultures: Bridging the Gap Between U.S. and Mexican Managers.* Yarmouth, ME: Intercultural Press, 1989.

Lenski, Gerard, and Jean Lenski. *Human Societies: An Introduction to Macrosociology.* New York: McGraw-Hill, 4th ed., 1982.

Leppert, Paul. *Doing Business with the Koreans: A Handbook for Executives.* Sebastopol, CA: Patton Pacific Press, 2nd ed., 1991.

Leppert, Paul. *Doing Business in Singapore: A Handbook for Executives.* Sebastopol, CA: Patton Pacific Press, 1990.

Leppert, Paul. *Doing Business with the Chinese: A Taiwan Handbook for Executives.* Sebastopol, CA: Patton Pacific Press, 1990.

LeVine, Robert A., and Donald T. Campbell. *Ethnocentrism: Theories of Conflict, Ethnic Attitudes and Group Behavior.* New York: John Wiley & Sons, 1972.

Lewis, Tom, and Robert Jungman. *On Being Foreign: Culture Shock in Short Fiction, An International Anthology.* Yarmouth, ME: Intercultural Press, 1986.

Loden, Marilyn, and Judy B. Rosener. *Work Force America!: Managing Employee Diversity as a Vital Resource.* Homewood, IL: Business One Irwin, 1990.

MacLeod, Roderick. *China, Inc.: How to Do Business with the Chinese.* New York: Bantam Books, 1988.

Marshall, Terry. *The Whole World Guide to Language Learning.* Yarmouth, ME: Intercultural Press, 1990.

Martin, Judith N., and Mitchell R. Hammer. "Behavioral Categories of Intercultural Communication Competence: Everyday Communicators' Perceptions." *International Journal of Intercultural Relations* 13, 3 (1989): 303-332.

Mead, Richard. *Cross-Cultural Management Communication.* New York: John Wiley & Sons, 1990.

Moran, Robert T. *Getting Your Yen's Worth: How to Negotiate with Japan, Inc.* Houston, TX: Gulf Publishing, 1984.

Moran, Robert T., and William G. Stripp. *Dynamics of Successful International Business Negotiations.* Houston, TX: Gulf Publishing, 1991.

Moran, Robert T., and Phillip R. Harris. *Managing Cultural Synergy.* Houston, TX: Gulf Publishing, 1982.

Moskowitz, M., R. Levering, and R. Katz. *Everybody's Business: A Field Guide to the 400 Leading Companies in America.* New York: Currency/Doubleday, 1990.

*National Trade Data Bank (NTDB): The Export Connection.* Washington, DC: U.S. Department of Commerce. CD-ROM; updated monthly.

Nierenberg, Gerard I. *The Complete Negotiator.* New York: Nierenberg & Zief Publishers, 1985.

Phillips-Martinsson, Jean. *Swedes as Others See Them: Facts, Myths or a Communication Complex.* Kent, England: Chartwell-Bratt, 1981. (Advice to Swedes working abroad as well as foreigners working in Sweden.)

Rearwin, David. *The Asia Business Book.* Yarmouth, ME: Intercultural Press, 1991.

Rhinesmith, Stephen H. *A Manager's Guide to Globalization: Six Keys to Success in a Changing World.* Homewood, IL: Business One Irwin, 1993.

Ricks, David A. *Big Business Blunders: Mistakes in International Marketing.* Homewood, IL: Dow-Jones Irwin, 1983.

Ricks, David A. and Michael R. Czinkota. "International Business: An Examination of the Corporate Viewpoint." *Journal of International Business Studies* (Fall 1979): 10:97-100.

Rubin, Joan, and Irene Thompson. *How to Be a More Successful Language Learner.* Boston: Heinle and Heinle, 1982.

Scott-Stevens, Susan. *Foreign Consultants and Counterparts: Problems in Technology Transfer.* Boulder, CO: Westview Press, 1987. (Case study of an Indonesian economic development project.)

Seelye, H. Ned. *Teaching Culture: Strategies for Intercultural Communication.* Lincolnwood, IL: National Textbook Co., 3rd rev. ed., 1993.

Seelye, H. Ned. "An Objective Measure of Biculturation: Americans in Guatemala, A Case Study." *Modern Language Journal* 53, 7 (Nov. 1969): 503-114.

Seelye, H. Ned, and Marilyn B. Brewer. "Ethnocentrism and Acculturation of North Americans in Guatemala." *Journal of Social Psychology* 80 (April 1970): 147-155.

Seelye, H. Ned, Edward C. P. Stewart, and Joyce A. Sween. *Evaluating Quality Circles in U.S. Industry*. Arlington, VA: Office of Naval Research, 1982. (NTIS: AD A118-649)

Shames, Germaine W., and Gerald W. Glover. *World-Class Service*. Yarmouth, ME: Intercultural Press, 1989. (For managers in international hospitality, travel, and tourism.)

Sieburg, Evelyn. Dysfunctional Communication and Interpersonal Responsiveness in Small Groups. (Unpublished doctoral dissertation.) University of Denver, 1969.

Simon, Paul. *The Tongue-Tied American: Confronting the Foreign Language Crisis*. New York: Continuum, 1980.

Simons, George F., Carmen Vázquez, and Phillip R. Harris. *Transcultural Leadership: Empowering the Diverse Workforce*. Houston, TX: Gulf Publishing Co., 1993.

Simons, George F. *Working Together: How to Become More Effective in a Multicultural Organization*. Los Altos, CA: Crisp Publications, 1989.

Stewart, Edward C., and Milton Bennett. *American Cultural Patterns: A Cross-Cultural Perspective*. Yarmouth, ME: Intercultural Press, 1991.

Sumner, William G. *Folkways*. New York: Ginn, 1906.

Theiderman, Sondra. *Bridging Cultural Barriers for Corporate Success: How to Manage the Multicultural Workforce*. Lexington, MA: Lexington Books, 1990.

Triandis, Harry C., et al. *The Analysis of Subjective Culture*. New York: Wiley-Interscience, 1972.

Triandis, Harry C., Richard Brislin, and C. Harry Hui. "Cross-Cultural Training Across the Individualism-Collectivism Divide." *International Journal of Intercultural Relations* 12, 3 (1988): 269-289.

Victor, David A. *International Business Communication*. New York: HarperCollins Publishers, 1992.

Weiss, Stephen E., and William Stripp. *Negotiating with Foreign Businesspersons*. New York: New York University Working Paper No. 1, February 1985.

The World Bank. *The World Bank Atlas 1994*. Washington, D.C.: The World Bank, 1994.

Zimmerman, Mark. *How to Do Business with the Japanese*. New York: Random House, 1985.

# Index

# About the Authors

**H. Ned Seelye** specializes in increasing the efficiency of organizations that deliver human services in multicultural settings. He has more than 25 years experience as an international consultant in Latin America, Europe, Asia, and Africa, and has managed multicultural workforces in the United States and Latin America.

When he was 16, Seelye left central Pennsylvania to seek his fortune in Mexico. Almost twenty years of his life unfolded in various countries abroad, including a two-year stint with NATO forces in Italy and ten years as a resident of Guatemala. He has taught in universities in six countries; in one, Ecuador, he was a senior Fulbright lecturer.

Seelye's undergraduate work was at the University of the Americas in Mexico and at Brigham Young University in Utah. He received a master's degree in Latin American studies from the fourth oldest university in the Western Hemisphere, la Universidad de San Carlos de Guatemala. Two additional years of graduate studies in anthropology at Tulane University of Louisiana and another year in social psychology at Northwestern University (Illinois) helped prepare him for the rigors of study in the School of Hard Knocks where he is still enrolled.

Seelye has published widely in professional journals (for example, *The Quality Circles Journal, International Journal of Quality & Reliability Management, Science Education, The Modern Language Journal, The Journal of Social Psychology*) and has written chapters for books published by houses such as Encyclopaedia Britannica, Intercultural Press, and Rand McNally. He has authored books published by several imprints of NTC Publishing Group. One of these, *Teaching Culture: Strategies for Intercultural Communication*, appeared in its third revised edition in 1993. Another book, co-authored with J. Laurence Day, appeared in 1992: *Careers for Foreign Language Aficionados & Other Multilingual Types*.

**Alan Seelye-James** is an industrial engineer (B.S., Northwestern University) who works as a manager for Kurt Salmon Associates, one of the world's leading management consultant firms specializing in the retail and consumer products industry. He has six years experience as a consultant to companies in Europe, Central Asia, Latin America, and the United States.

Seelye-James, born in Guatemala, was raised mostly in the United States, with prolonged visits to various Latin American countries. Besides English and Spanish, he is fluent in Russian (he has studied at the Moscow Energy Institute and has worked on projects in Russia) and is functional in Portuguese. (All four languages came in handy at a factory in New Jersey.)